KU-771-720

THE TRUE BOUNDS OF CHRISTIAN
FREEDOM

The True Bounds of Christian Freedom

SAMUEL BOLTON

THE BANNER OF TRUTH TRUST

THE BANNER OF TRUTH TRUST
3 Murrayfield Road, Edinburgh EH12 6EL
P.O. Box 621, Carlisle, Pennsylvania 17013, U.S.A.

★

First published 1645
First Banner of Truth Trust edition 1964

Reprinted 1978

ISBN 0 85151 083 3

The Publishers wish to record their gratitude to the late
Rev. J. Marcellus Kik of Silver Spring, Maryland,
U.S.A., for his advice and encouragement in the pre-
paration of this edition of *The True Bounds of
Christian Freedom*.

PRINTED AND BOUND IN GREAT BRITAIN BY
HAZELL WATSON AND VINEY LTD, AYLESBURY, BUCKS

CONTENTS

THE discovery of gold has excited men throughout history to make considerable sacrifices and to endure heroic hardships. Without sacrifice and hardship gold could not have been mined. One of the exciting discoveries of recent times is the large store of spiritual gold contained in the writings of the Reformers and Puritans of the sixteenth and seventeenth centuries. To mine the gold certainly requires some labour and effort, but it is exceedingly rewarding. The reprinting of Samuel Bolton's work on Christian freedom provides the reader with an opportunity to enrich himself with nuggets to which the words of Genesis might well be applied, 'The gold of that land is good'. Bolton was sufficiently renowned in Puritan England as a scholar and divine, to be chosen as one of the Westminster Assembly of Divines which met in 1643 to introduce a second Reformation in English religion.

The theme of Christian liberty continues to be a subject of lively discussion and debate in many circles. Some would remove everything which would restrict, circumscribe, or confine freedom. Christian liberty, it is maintained, must not be restricted by law—not only that revealed by Moses but even the maxims and precepts of Christ revealed in the New Testament. There must be no flavour of legalism or moralism, they say, if 'liberty in Christ' is to be preserved in the Church.

This plea is specious but false, and Bolton ably exposes its fallacies. The thrust of the work, although apparent from the original sub-title—'A Treatise wherein the rights of the law are vindicated, the liberties of grace maintained'—is stated fully in the Dedication: 'It contains chiefly some friendly discussion of some opinions which have been maintained against the law of God, and in it I have endeavoured to uphold the law so as to show that it does not take from the liberties of grace, and to establish grace so that the law is not made void, and so that believers are not set free from any duty they owe to God or man.'[1]

Those who would exclude the law because it seems to infringe on the freedom of the Christian claim that the whole of the New Testament maintains a creative tension between law and gospel. Bolton points out rightly that any tension or opposition between law and Gospel is chiefly of man's own making. Obedience to the moral law, revealed in both Old and New Testaments, need not necessarily lead to what Bolton calls 'legal obedience'; there is a free and evangelical obedience.

An unbalanced emphasis on grace has led men to neglect certain of the law's various functions. In its accusing and convicting function, the law is a schoolmaster to lead men to Christ. The absence of this dimension in the preaching of today has resulted in a truncated Gospel, rushed conversion work and a shallow religious experience. The law prepares the way for the Gospel and 'a man can never preach the Gospel that makes not way for the Gospel'.

Grievous and alarming is the present-day deterioration in the moral condition of society. For this decay the Church is partly blameworthy because, as the preserving salt of the community, she has largely lost her savour. Modern theology has defected. It has cut itself adrift from the ancient landmarks, and present-day society reaps 'the evil thing and bitter' which is the inevitable consequence. The present prevailing theology has not been able to elevate society and halt its moral decline, and unquestionably, one explanation of this is its misunderstanding of the place of the law and its usefulness in

[1]For a modern discussion of the historical and theological background to this treatise, see *The Grace of Law*, E. F. Kevan, London 1963, and reprinted in 1976 by Baker Book House, Grand Rapids, U.S.A.

the service of the covenant of grace. The Church needs to know again the truth of Bolton's statement: 'The law sends us to the Gospel for our justification; the Gospel sends us to the law to frame our way of life.'

Samuel Bolton, the author of this treatise on Christian liberty, was born in London in 1606, and educated at Christ's College, Cambridge, where he became a Doctor of Divinity. He was successively minister in three London parishes before becoming Master of Christ's College in 1645. Six years later we find him serving the University of Cambridge as Vice-Chancellor. After a long illness he died in 1654. In his will he instructed his executors that he was 'to be interred as a private Christian, and not with the outward pomp of a doctor, because he hoped to rise in the day of judgment and appear before God, not as a doctor, but as a humble Christian'. His funeral sermon was preached by Dr Edmund Calamy.

Five works came from Bolton's pen between 1644 and 1647, and two others were published after his death. The second of the seven was *The True Bounds of Christian Freedom*, which appeared in 1645 under the Imprimatur of John Downame, who had been appointed as a Puritan 'licenser of the press'. Downame describes it as a 'solid, judicious, pious and very profitable' discourse.

The original work is utterly formless and styleless. There are no chapter breaks and paragraphing hardly exists. Instead, there are divisions, sub-divisions and sub-sub-divisions which tantalize even the serious reader. Nor is there the slightest attempt to cultivate the grace of style. In this reprint, therefore, an attempt has been made to rectify certain of these faults. Credit for this belongs to S. M. Houghton, M.A., of Oxford. Sentences have frequently been redrafted to fulfil the requirements of clarity and simplicity, and an approach to modern paragraphing has been introduced. There has been no attempt, however, to alter Bolton's personal non-literary style. Had this been attempted the book could no longer be claimed as from his pen. A framework has been supplied and numbered divisions and sub-divisions have in some cases been eliminated. A new and simplified table of contents replaces the original table which in its complexity resembled a maze.

It should not be thought that in this treatise Christian liberty is treated in a cold, analytical fashion. Warmth and devotion to Christ mark all its pages. The slur of 'legalism' often cast upon those who framed the Westminster Confession of Faith finds no justification in this instructive and edifying work. Bolton's treatise represents a combination of doctrinal and experimental theology which aims at touching the conscience even as it enlightens the understanding. It avoids intemperate language, and attempts to see the points at issue in their true relationship with the main body of Reformation and Puritan doctrine, and especially with the theology of the covenants. The diligent reader will indeed be rewarded with much spiritual treasure as he explores and mines in this Puritan Eldorado.

TO THE CHRISTIAN READER

It is well known that, just as God has communicated many truths to man, so has Satan endeavoured to bring in many errors, his hope being to prejudice and weaken the reception of the truth even though he failed to induce men to entertain his lies. Indeed he finds that his best time for selling his wares is when pedlars are most busy, and when, in the busy market, men are buying truth. It is then that he offers his merchandise. To make it more vendible he represents it as highly respectable and as spiritual in character as truth itself. For long he has walked as a prince of darkness, but because he has lost hope of deceiving men any longer as such, he now transforms himself into an angel of light. Successful in past ages as a bare-faced deceiver, he put on a mask when men discovered his real character, and thus disguised he carried on his designs for generations. But the mask is now taken off, and he operates as one wearing the very face of truth.

No errors are more dangerous and destructive than those which reach men as the teachings of free grace. Poison in the fountain from which they spring, they are poison in men's hearts. I need not tell how many of them have been brought before men and received by them. For the recovery of those who have been thus carried away, for the establishing of those who stagger, and for the upbuilding of those who are in some measure settled in the truth, the following treatise is, at the request of many friends who heard it preached, now printed. It is partly doctrinal, setting forth and confirming the truth commonly received by Christians, and partly controversial, examining and confuting the contrary opinions.

We have given our opponents a fair trial, having been willing to hear the utmost they could say. Our examination of the questions on which we differ is comprised under six queries, namely,

1. *Whether our being made free by Christ frees us from the law,*
2. *Whether our being made free by Christ delivers us from all punishments or chastisements for sin,*
3. *Whether it is consistent with Christian freedom to be under obligation to perform duties because God has commanded them,*
4. *Whether Christ's freemen may come into bondage again through sin,*
5. *Whether it is consistent with Christian freedom to perform duties out of respect for the recompense of the reward,*
6. *Whether the freedom of a Christian frees him from all obedience to men.*

These will be the main inquiries. Opinions contrary to those here expounded will be debated in a friendly manner and plainly confuted. My main aim is to convince the judgment, not to irritate the affections, lest while I seek to be helpful to grace, I might render service to sin, and while I endeavour to lead men to holiness, I should stir up men's corruptions, and so run in vain. I have sought, therefore, to deal with principles more than persons, and rather to unveil errors by means of argument than by naming them. It is my earnest desire that what is here made obvious to the eye, the God of truth would make evident to the heart, and that He would give to my readers and myself sound judgment, that we may be able to distinguish between things that differ. May He guide us in the ways of faith and obedience, enable us to serve Him while we live, smile upon us when we die, and after death take us to Himself. This is all I desire for myself, and the least I desire for my readers.

Yours in the service of Christ, to
advance faith and obedience,
SAMUEL BOLTON.

April 23, 1645.

I

TRUE CHRISTIAN FREEDOM

*'If the Son therefore shall make you free, ye shall
be free indeed'* (John 8.36).

It is set down as a part of the sufferings of Christ (Heb. 12.3)
that He endured the contradiction of sinners. And among all
the chapters in the Gospel there is none that sets down so great
a part of the sufferings of Christ in this respect as this eighth
chapter of John. From the twelfth verse to the end of the
chapter almost every verse shows how the Jews set the pride of
their obstinate and rebellious wills against His Divine and in-
finite wisdom. There was nothing that Christ could speak but
their rebellious hearts cavilled at it, and sought to thwart and
contradict Him in it. Yet there were some among them that
the Word had better effects upon. In verse 31 it is recorded
that, though there were many to contradict, yet some were
wrought upon, some believed. To those in particular Christ
directs Himself, by way of caution and encouragement, and
tells them that if they continued in His word, they would know
the truth; yea, and the truth would make them free.

Whereupon the Jews answered (not those that believed, as
appears by verse 37, for the same persons that thus answered
sought to kill Him): 'We be Abraham's seed, and were never
in bondage to any man: how sayest thou, Ye shall be made
free?' Christ might have returned this impudent cavil upon
them by urging them to review their former state under the
Egyptians and Babylonians, and their present condition under
the Romans; but putting aside their political bondage, He

proves them to be in spiritual and soul bondage to sin. 'He that committeth sin is the servant of sin' (v. 34); and you, said He, commit sin.

Having shown them their present sinful condition, He next goes on to tell them what would be their future doom. They must be cast out of the house, although they were now in the Church of God. As the apostle says: 'Cast out the bond-woman and her son'. This Christ proves by contrasting the condition of a servant and of a son: 'The servant abideth not in the house for ever: but the Son abideth ever' (v. 35). Yet He does not leave them here under their sad doom, but propounds to them a way to prevent it, namely, by endeavouring to get free. He then sets down the means by which this freedom may be obtained, and that is by the Son. Though the work is difficult, yet He that abides in the house for ever, He that is the Son, can effect it: 'For if the Son shall make you free, ye shall be free indeed'.

Thus have I shown you how my text is related to, and depends upon, the preceding words. We shall now look at the text as it stands complete in itself: 'If the Son shall make you free –'

Here we observe, first, a supposition – 'If the Son shall make you free'; secondly, a consequence – 'Ye shall be free indeed'. Give me leave to set forth this truth in four particulars:

First, We have a benefit expressed – freedom: 'If the Son shall make you *free*'.

Secondly, We have the qualities of this freedom – it is a true and real freedom: 'free *indeed*'.

Thirdly, We have the subjects of this freedom – believers: 'If the Son shall make *you* free'.

Fourthly, We have the author of it – Christ: 'If *the Son* shall make you free'.

From what is expressed and what is implied, we can draw four conclusions:

(1) That every man by nature, and in the state of nature, is in bondage,

(2) That some are set free from this bondage,

(3) That those who are set free are set free by Christ,

(4) That such as Christ sets free are free indeed.

I do not propose to deal with all these matters in this discourse: it will not suit my present purpose. Not that the subject of the bondage of men might not be of service, as set in contrast with spiritual freedom. Much can be learned from contraries. Just as something of heaven is to be known from the consideration of hell, so something of the excellency of spiritual freedom may be known from the consideration of man's natural bondage—a bondage to sin, to Satan, and to the law of God. All which is a universal bondage of the soul, a cruel bondage, a willing bondage, a bondage out of which we are not able to redeem ourselves by ransom, or to deliver ourselves by our own power.

The doctrine of man's bondage we shall not at present expound further, though I may make some application of it later. The four points about freedom, however, on which I shall now speak, I will sum up in one statement of doctrine: *That there is a true and real freedom which Christ has purchased, and into which He has brought all those who are true believers.* This is the teaching of the text. Otherwise stated, we have here the nature, the quality, and the parts of Christian freedom.

THE NATURE OF CHRISTIAN FREEDOM

First, we shall consider the nature of this freedom.

There are four kinds of freedom—natural, political, sensual, and spiritual. Natural freedom is that which is enjoyed by everything in nature, but this is not the freedom intended in the text. Political freedom pertains to a Nation, a State, a

Commonwealth, a Corporation, and it was of this that the Jews understood Christ to speak. They were Abraham's seed, and therefore free. But Christ did not speak of this. Again, there is a corrupt and sinful freedom which we express under the name of Libertinism. To this the apostle refers in Gal. 5.13: 'Brethren, ye are called unto liberty: but use not liberty as an occasion to the flesh', that is, as an occasion to sin. It is a fearful thing when men turn the grace of God into wantonness. Such men are spoken of in the fourth verse of the Epistle of Jude: 'There are certain men crept in unawares, who were before of old ordained to this condemnation, ungodly men, turning the grace of our God into lasciviousness'. Perhaps they reasoned thus: 'Let us abound in sin because God has abounded in grace' (Rom. 6), which is fearful reasoning, not that of a child of God. Of the same sort of men, the apostle Peter speaks (1 Pet. 2.16): 'As free, and not using your liberty for a cloke of maliciousness' (that is to say, as a pretext or a colour to sin), 'but as the servants of God'. It is evil to sin, to do any act of maliciousness, but much more so to cloak or cover it; and much more again to make Christian liberty the cloak of sin: that is most damnable. To make religion, to make the truth of God, to make Christian liberty so dearly purchased, a cloak or pretext to sin, or to take occasion to sin by it, is a fearful sin.

But of this Christ does not here speak. This is our bondage, not our freedom, as I shall show later.

It is a spiritual and heavenly freedom of which our text speaks, a freedom purchased by Christ, revealed in the Gospel, and conveyed to the saints of God as the great dowry of Christ to His Church and Spouse. Two great things Christ has entrusted into the hands of His Church—Christian faith and Christian liberty. Just as we are to contend earnestly for the maintenance of the faith (Jude 3), so also for the maintenance of Christian liberty, and that against all who would oppose and undermine it: 'Stand fast therefore in the liberty wherewith Christ hath made us free' (Gal. 5.1). Very like this is the exhortation of the same apostle: 'Ye are bought with a price: be not ye the servants of men' (1 Cor. 7.23). But of this I shall say more hereafter.

In general, then, I say, the freedom into which Christ brings believers is a spiritual, a Divine freedom, a freedom contrasted with their former bondage. If this is clearly understood it will explain what Christian freedom really is.

THE QUALITY OF CHRISTIAN FREEDOM

We come next to inquire what is the quality of this freedom. One quality is mentioned in the text; I shall add two more to it. First, it is a real freedom, not an imaginary or fancied freedom. Too many imagine themselves to be free who are really in bondage. But this is no imaginary freedom; it is a freedom indeed, a true and real freedom. Whom the Son makes free are free indeed.

Again, it is a universal freedom, a freedom which does not leave us partially in bondage. Christian liberty frees a believer from all kinds of previous bondage. But we must beware of taking any part of our liberty for our bondage, or of our bondage for our liberty. Too many do so. We were, then, in bondage to Satan, to sin, to the law, to wrath, to death, to hell. By this privilege we are freed from all. It is a universal freedom, universal in respect of persons – believers; universal in respect of its parts. We are free from all that was, or is any way part of our bondage; free from Satan, from sin, from the law, as I shall show later.

Then, too, it is a constant freedom; a Christian is brought into a condition of freedom, a state of freedom, as previously he was in a state of bondage. Wherever the Lord's jubilee is proclaimed and pronounced in a man's soul, he will never hear again of a return to bondage. He will never again come under bondage to Satan, the law, or aught else. This is implied by

Christ in the words: 'The servant abideth not in the house for ever; but the Son abideth ever' (John 8.35). The apostle expresses the same truth under the figure of an allegory when he says: 'Abraham had two sons, the one by a bondmaid, the other by a freewoman' (Gal. 4.22). Here he distinguishes between those who are under the law, and those who are under the Gospel, the children of the bondwoman and those of the free, the heirs of promise and the servants of the law. The one must be cast out, says Paul. Likewise Christ speaks here: 'The servant abides not in the house for ever' (they shall not inherit) 'but the Son abides in the house for ever.' The sons shall inherit, shall enjoy a perpetual freedom, and shall never again return to bondage.

THE BRANCHES OF CHRISTIAN FREEDOM

We come now to consider the third thing propounded, the branches of this Christian freedom. But before I speak of this, I must necessarily tell you that freedom in general has two branches. First, there is inchoate freedom, that is, the freedom we enjoy during the days of our pilgrimage, freedom in grace; second, consummate freedom, that is, the freedom of our Father's house, freedom in glory. We shall speak chiefly of the first – inchoate freedom.

FREEDOM IN ITS NEGATIVE ASPECTS

(i) *Freedom from Satan*

To begin with, it is clear that believers are free from Satan. Christ has wrested us and delivered us from Satan's hands. We were prisoners to Satan, in his chains, and Christ has brought us deliverance. This is set down by way of a parable in the Gospel of Luke: 'When a strong man armed keepeth his palace, his goods are in peace: but when a stronger than he shall come upon him, and overcome him, he taketh from him all his armour wherein he trusted, and divideth his spoils' (ch. 11.21–22). But it is plainly stated in Heb. 2.14, 15: Christ came into the world 'that through death he might destroy him that had the power of death, that is, the devil'. Christ freed us from the wrath of God, from the devil's power, by purchase. By a strong hand He delivers us from Satan, just as He delivered the children of Israel out of Egypt by a strong hand.

(ii) *Freedom from Sin*

Secondly, we are freed from sin, by which I mean the guilt, the defilement and the dominion of sin. That none of our sins shall condemn us or bring wrath upon us, Christ interposes Himself between us and wrath, so that no one shall be able to condemn us: 'There is therefore now no condemnation to them which are in Christ Jesus' (Rom. 8.1). Christ Himself shall as soon be called to account for your sin as you yourself. If you have an interest in Him, sin shall never condemn you, for Christ has made satisfaction for it. 'Those whose standing is in Christ have made satisfaction in Christ to all the requirements of God and His law' (Piscator).

It would not be righteous of God to require payment from Christ, nay, to receive the full satisfaction of Christ, and to require anything from you. This is what God has done: 'He laid on him the iniquity of us all' (Isa. 53.6). This is what Christ has done: He paid God till God said He had enough. He was fully satisfied, fully contented: 'This is my beloved Son, in whom I am well pleased' (Matt. 3.17 and 12.18), that is, 'in whom I am fully satisfied and appeased'. Hence the apostle writes: 'God was in Christ, reconciling the world unto Himself . . . for he hath made him to be sin for us, who knew no sin; that we might be made the righteousness of God in him' (2 Cor. 5.19–21). God was paying Himself out of the blood, scourgings, and sufferings of Christ; and in that, Christ made a full payment. Hence Christ says: 'I send my Spirit, and he will convince the world, as of sin so of righteousness, because I go to the Father and ye see me no more' (John 16.7–10). That is, you shall see Me no more after this fashion. You shall never see Me again as a sufferer, as a satisfier of God's justice for sin. I have completed this work. Indeed we should have seen Christ again if He had not satisfied justice. If the guilt of but one of those sins He bore had remained on Him unsatisfied for, it would have held Him under chains of death and the power of the grave for ever. He could never have risen, much less ascended and gone to the Father, if He had not met the claims of justice to the full. For this reason the apostle throws down a challenge. He sets the death of Christ against whatever sin, Satan, justice, and the law can say: 'Who shall lay anything to the charge of God's elect? It is God that justifieth. Who is he that condemneth? It is Christ that died, yea rather, that is risen again, who is even at the right hand of God, who also maketh intercession for us' (Rom. 8.33–34). He does not say, Who shall accuse? but, Who shall condemn? Indeed, we may have accusers enough – sin, Satan, conscience, and the rest – but none can condemn. The issues of life and death are not in their hand. And as none of our sins shall condemn us, so none of our sins shall ever bring us into a state of condemnation again, ever put us under the curse or under wrath again.

Likewise, none of our sins can bring upon us the consequences of Divine wrath. We are freed from all miseries, calamities, afflictions, and punishments which are the fruits of sin, so far as they have wrath in them. If you take away the substance, the shadow must needs depart also. Sin is the substance, punishment the shadow that attends it and follows it. Take away sin and then the punishments are also taken away. All God's dispensations are in mercy.

It is agreed by all that eternal punishments can never come upon any of those whom Christ has freed from sin, those whom He has justified. From other punishments that have something of eternal punishment in them, believers are also freed. Nothing in the nature of Divine wrath can touch them.

I grant that God does afflict those whose sin He pardons, but there is a great deal of difference in respect of the hand from which the afflictions proceed, the persons who bear the afflictions, the reasons for afflicting, and the ends that God aims at in sending the afflictions, as I shall show later.

It is clear that, so far as afflictions are part of the curse for sin, God does not and cannot afflict His people for sin. Nor does God afflict His people for sin as if such afflictions were payments or satisfactions for sin, and as if God's justice was not fully satisfied for sin by Christ; as if Christ had left something for us to bear by way of satisfaction. The Papists say this (and therefore they perform penances and punish themselves) but so do not we.

Again, so far as afflictions are the sole fruits of sin, God does not bring them upon His people, for in this respect they are part of the curse. Afflictions upon wicked men are penal, a part of the curse; there is nothing medicinal in them; they are the effects of vindictive justice and not of Fatherly mercy. But afflictions which come upon the godly are medicinal in purpose, and are intended to cure them of sin.

Whether, then, we have regard to punishment eternal, spiritual, or temporal, Christ has freed the godly from all : from eternal punishment as the wrath which is due to sin, from spiritual punishment as it is related to eternal, and from temporal as far as it is related to both the others, and as far as it has anything of God's wrath in it.

God has thoughts of love in all He does to His people. The ground of His dealings with us is love (though the occasion may be sin), the manner of His dealings is love, and the purpose of His dealings is love. He has regard, in all, to our good here, to make us partakers of His holiness, and to our glory hereafter, to make us partakers of His glory.

But it is not so in regard to God's punishment of wicked men. Neither is the ground love, nor the manner love, nor the purpose love. All His dealings with them in this respect are parts of the curse and have regard to the demerit of their sin.

Christ has also freed the believer from the dominion of sin: 'Sin shall not have dominion over you' (Rom. 6.14). Why? 'For ye are not under the law, but under grace'. Indeed, while we were under the law, sin had full dominion. It had not only possession of us, but dominion over us. And that dominion was a voluntary, a willing, a free subjection and resignation of ourselves to the motions and services of sin. Then we went down stream, wind, and tide. There was both the power of lust, and lustful inclinations, to carry us: this was the tide, the other was the wind. But now, being under grace, a covenant of grace, and being interested in Christ and set free by Him, we are freed from the dominion and power of sin.

We still have the presence of sin, nay, the stirrings and workings of corruptions. These make us to have many a sad heart and wet eye. Yet Christ has thus far freed us from sin; it shall not have dominion. There may be the turbulence, but not the prevalence of sin. There may be the stirrings of corruption. It was said of Carthage that Rome was more troubled with it when half destroyed than when whole. So a godly man may be more troubled with sin when it is conquered than when it reigned. Sin will still work, but it is checked in its workings. They are rather workings for life than from life. They are not such uncontrolled workings as formerly. Sin is under command. Indeed, it may get advantage, and may have a tyranny in the soul, but it will never more be sovereign. I say, it may get into the throne of the heart and play the tyrant in this or that particular act of sin, but it shall never more be as a king there. Its reign is over; you will never yield a voluntary obedience to sin. Sin is conquered, though it still has a being within you.

Augustine describes man under four different conditions. Before the law he neither fights nor strives against sin. Under the law he fights but is overcome. Under grace he fights and conquers. But in heaven it is all conquest, and there is no combat more to all eternity. It is our happiness here in grace that there is a conquest, though a daily combat: we fight, but we get the victory; sin shall nevermore have dominion over us. Those sins that were kings are now captives in us; sins that were in the throne are now in chains. What a mercy is this! Others are under the authoritative commands of every passion, of every lust; every sin has command over them; no temptation comes but it conquers. A sinful heart stands ready to entertain every sin that comes with power; it is taken captive at pleasure and with pleasure.

But the believer is free from the dominion of sin. In temptation sin is broken. There is no allowing of sin in the understanding. The soul is not willing to allow of sin as sin under any shape or form. There is no closing with it in the will, no embracing of it in the affections. Its workings are broken and wounded. O believers, you will never be willing captives to sin again; you may be captives, never subjects; sin may tyrannize, never reign. The reign of sin describes a soul under the power of sin and in a state of sin. But sin rather dies than lives in you. A sickly man who is pining away is said rather to be dying than living; to live implies a getting of strength, and sin does not do this. It is in a consumptive state, dying daily.

Sin is dead judicially; Christ has sentenced it. Christ has condemned sin in the flesh (Rom. 8.3). Sin met its death blow in the death of Christ. And it is dying actually. As was the case with the house of Saul, it is decreasing every day. But notice that God has chosen to put sin to a lingering death, to a death upon the cross, and this for the greater punishment of sin, that it might die gradually. But also, it is for the further humiliation of saints that they might be put upon the exercise of prayer and cast upon the hold of their faith. It is intended to exercise their faith for the daily breaking of the power of sin and corruption in them.

Thus much then upon our deliverance from sin by Christ.

(iii) *Freedom from the Law*

Christ has freed us from the law: that is another part of our freedom by Christ. 'Ye are delivered from the law, that being dead wherein we were held; that we should serve in newness of spirit, and not in the oldness of the letter' (Rom. 7.6). 'I through the law am dead to the law, that I might live unto God' (Gal. 2.19). 'If ye be led by the Spirit, ye are not under the law' (Gal. 5.18). 'Ye are not under the law, but under grace' (Rom. 6.14). This then is another part of our freedom by Christ: we are freed from the law. What this is we shall now consider.

We are freed from the ceremonial law, which was a yoke which neither we nor our fathers were able to bear (Acts 15.10). Yet this is but a small part of our freedom.

(a) *Freedom from the law as a covenant*

We are freed from the moral law: freed from it, first, as a covenant, say our divines. It would save a great deal of trouble to say we are freed from the law as that from which life might be expected on the condition that due obedience was rendered. But take it, as do many, in the sense that we are freed from the law as a covenant.

The law may be considered as a rule and as a covenant. When we read that the law is still in force, it is to be understood of the law as a rule, not as a covenant. Again, when we read that the law is abrogated, and that we are freed from the law, it is to be understood of the law as a covenant, not as a rule. But yet in all this it is not yet expressed what covenant it is. The apostle calls it the old covenant (Heb. 8.13) under which they were, and from which we are freed. It could never give us life; it cannot now inflict death on us. We are dead to it, and it is now dead to us. We read in Romans 7.1–6: 'The law hath dominion over a man as long as he liveth. For the woman which hath an husband is bound by the law to her husband as long as he liveth; but if the husband be dead, she is loosed from the law of her husband.' Among other interpretations which might be set down, I shall suggest this one only: the law is your husband; you are under subjection to it as you are looking by your subjection to be justified and saved. And until the law as a covenant or husband is dead to you, and you to it (for the apostle makes them both one), you will never look for righteousness and life in another. Until the law kills you, and you are dead to it, you will look for righteousness and life through obedience to it. But when once the law has killed you, and showed you it is dead to you and can do you no good, so that you can expect nothing from it, then will you look for life by Christ alone.

Such was the apostle's own case. He was once one that expected (as well he might) as much good from the law and his obedience to it as any man. Says he: 'I was alive without the law once: but when the commandment came, sin revived and I died. And the commandment, which was ordained to life, I found to be unto death' (Rom. 7.9, 10). That is to say, I found that instead of saving me it killed me; it gave death instead of life. And again he says: 'For sin, taking occasion by the commandment, deceived me, and by it slew me': that is, the law came in with an enlightening, convincing, accusing, condemning power, and laid me on my back, and did clean kill me. I saw I could expect nothing there, nothing from it as a covenant.

As for the apostle, therefore, the law was now dead to him, and could afford him nothing; likewise was he also dead to the law. He expected nothing from it afterwards. As he tells us later: 'I through the law am dead to the law, that I might live unto God' (Gal. 2.19): that is, the law having now slain me, I am for ever dead to it. I expect nothing from it as a covenant; all my life is in Christ. I look now to live by another. I through the law, that is, through the convincing, enlightening, condemning, killing power of it, see that it is dead to me and I to it. I can expect nothing from it, that is, as a covenant of life and death. It is dead to me and I to it, and I look for all from Christ.

Thus are we freed from the law as a covenant. I shall speak more largely of this in the answers to the queries later. Meanwhile we come to deal with other branches of our Christian freedom from the law, the next in order being our freedom from the maledictions and curses of the law.

(b) Freedom from the curses of the law

The law requires two things of them who are under it: either they must obey the precepts, which is impossible with the degree of strictness and rigidness which the law requires (Gal. 3); or they must bear the penalties of the law, which are insupportable. Either they must obey the commands or suffer the curses of the law, either do God's will or suffer God's will in forfeitures of soul and body. In this sad dilemma are those who are under the law as a covenant: 'He that believeth not is condemned already . . . the wrath of God abideth on him' (John 3.18, 36). Unbelievers must needs be under the curses of the law.

But believers are freed from the law as a covenant of life and death. Therefore they are free from the curses and maledictions of the law. The law has nothing to do with them as touching their eternal state and condition. Hence the words of the apostle: 'There is therefore now no condemnation to them which are in Christ Jesus' (Rom. 8.1), that is, to them who are not under the law. Were you indeed under the law as a covenant, condemnation would meet you, nothing else but condemnation. Though the law is not able to save you, yet it is able to condemn you. Unable to bestow the blessing, yet it can pour the curse upon you: 'As many as are of the works of the law' – that is, those under the law as a covenant, and that look for life and justification thereby – 'are under the curse' (Gal. 3.10). And he continues with the argument: 'For it is written,

Cursed is everyone that continueth not in all things which are written in the book of the law to do them'. It is not possible for a man to obey in all things without failing in any; hence he is left under the curse. So that I say, if you are under the law, the law is able to condemn you, though it cannot save you (Rom. 8.3).

But Christ has brought freedom to those in Him, freedom from the curses of the law, and that by bearing this curse for them, as it is written: 'Christ hath redeemed us from the curse of the law, being made a curse for us' (Gal. 3.13). The apostle not only says that Christ bore the curse for us, but that He was made a curse for us, for: 'It is written, Cursed is every one that hangeth on a tree'. This is another of the benefits which flow from Christ's work. The believer is freed from the law as a covenant, and so from the curse of the law. The law cannot pass sentence upon him, it cannot condemn him. He is not to be tried in that court. Christ has satisfied the law to the full.

This privilege belongs not only to the present; it lasts for ever. Even though the believer falls into sin, yet the law cannot pronounce the curse on him because, as he is not under the law, he is freed from the curse of the law. A man is never afraid of that obligation which is rendered void, the seals torn off, the writing defaced, nay, not only crossed out and cancelled but torn in pieces. It is thus that God has dealt with the law in the case of believers, as touching its power to curse them, to sentence them and condemn. The apostle tells us: 'He hath blotted out the handwriting of ordinances that was against us, which was contrary to us, and took it out of the way, nailing it to his cross' (Col. 2.14). By 'the handwriting of ordinances' I conceive is not meant the ceremonial law alone, but the moral law also, so far as it was against us and bound us over to the curse.

We can here observe the successive steps which the apostle sets out. 'He hath blotted out.' But lest this should not be enough, lest any should say, It is not so blotted out, but it may be read, the apostle adds, 'He took it out of the way'. But lest even this should not be enough, lest some should say, Yea, but it will be found again and set against us afresh, he adds, 'nailing it to his cross'. He has torn it to pieces, never to be put together again for ever. It can never be that the law has a claim against believers on account of their sins. Indeed it brings in black bills, strong indictments against such as are under it; but it shall never have anything to produce against those who have an interest in Christ. I may say of believers, as the apostle does in another sense, 'Against such there is no law'. As there is no law to justify them, so there is no law to condemn them.

Five reasons why the law cannot condemn the believer

All this the apostle puts plainly: 'Who is he that condemneth? it is Christ that died' (Rom. 8.34). He sets the death of Christ against all the charges that can be brought. It is evident that the court of the law cannot condemn the believer:

(1) Because that court is itself condemned; its curses, judgments, and sentences are made invalid. As men that are condemned have a tongue but no voice, so the law in this case has still a tongue to accuse, but no power to condemn. It cannot fasten condemnation on the believer.

(2) Because he is not under it as a court. He is not under the law as a covenant of life and death. As he is in Christ, he is under the covenant of grace.

(3) Because he is not subject to its condemnation. He is under its guidance, but not under its curses, under its precepts (though not on the legal condition of 'Do this and live'), but not under its penalties.

(4) Because Christ, in his place and stead, was condemned by it that he might be freed: 'Christ hath redeemed us

from the curse of the law, being made a curse for us' (Gal. 3.13). It may condemn sin in us, but cannot condemn us for sin.

(5) Because he has appealed from it. We see this in the case of the publican, who was arrested, dragged into the court of justice, sentenced and condemned. But this has no force because he makes his appeal, 'God be merciful to me a sinner' (Luke 18.13). He flies to Christ, and, says the text, 'He went down to his house justified'. So the court of the law (provided that your appeal is just) cannot condemn, because you have appealed to the court of mercy.

True and false appeals from the court of the law

Indeed there are many who make a false appeal. They appeal in part, not wholly, for they trust partly on Christ and partly on themselves. Many appeal to Christ for salvation who do not appeal to Him for sanctification. This is false. Many appeal to Christ before they are brought into the court of the law, before they are humbled, convinced, and condemned by the law. The case of the publican shows what kind of appeal will do a man good. Condemned in the court of the law, he makes his appeal to Christ in the Gospel. Read the words spoken of him : 'He stood afar off, and would not lift up so much as his eyes unto heaven, but smote upon his breast, saying, God be merciful to me a sinner'. Here was a threefold demeanour, answering to a threefold work within him. First, he stood afar off; this answers to his fear and consternation. Then, he would not so much as lift up his eyes; this answers to his shame and confusion. Again, he smote his breast; this answers to his sorrow and compunction. And being in such a case he then appeals : 'God be merciful to me a sinner'.

In brief, then, if your appeal is a right one and such as will do you good, it must be a total, not a partial, appeal. You must not come to Christ for some relief only, but for all.

Christ must have the honour of all. Also, it must be an appeal for grace as well as mercy, for sanctification as well as salvation, an appeal to be made holy by Christ as well as to be made happy by Christ. Again, it must be the appeal of a man humbled and condemned in himself. No man will appeal to another court until he is found guilty and condemned in the former. So here, we cannot appeal to Christ until first we are found guilty and condemned by Moses. This the apostle shows: 'We have proved both Jews and Gentiles to be all under sin; as it is written, There is none righteous, no, not one; there is none that understandeth, none that seeketh after God' (Rom. 3.9–11).

Thus runs the indictment and the accusation of the law, and in verse 19 is found the sentence or judgment upon it, and there the apostle tells us the reason why the law says this: 'That every mouth may be stopped, and all the world may become guilty before God'. It is when the law has accused and sentenced us, when it has stopped our mouths and we become guilty, that the sinner comes to make his appeal from the law as a covenant to Christ as a Saviour. He looks for nothing from justice, but all from mercy. And when he has thus appealed, the law has no more to do with him; he is not under the sentence, the penalties of the law; he is out of the law's reach. The law can take no hold of him for condemnation; he has fled to Christ, and taken sanctuary in Him.

What a privilege is this, to be free from the curses and penalties of the law, so that if the law threatens, Christ promises; if the law curses, Christ blesses. This is a high privilege. If God did but let one spark of His wrath and displeasure fall upon your conscience for sin, you would then know what a mercy it is to be thus freed.

(c) Freedom from the accusations of the law

But now we proceed to consider the freedom which the believer has from the indictments and accusations of the law:

'Who shall lay anything to the charge of God's elect?' (Rom. 8.33). This may be thought a strange question, 'who shall?', but there are several such accusers:

Satan is ready to lay things to their charge. He is called 'the accuser of the saints . . . night and day' (Rev. 12.10). He is the great Calumniator, ever bringing forward bills of indictment against the saints. Sometimes he accuses God to man, as in the case of our first parents, where he charged God with envy to His creatures, as if He had forbidden the tree lest they should become too wise. It is ordinary with Satan, either to accuse God's mercy by telling men they may sin and yet God will be merciful, or to accuse His justice by saying that, if they sin, there is no mercy for them. As he stretches God's justice above the bounds of the Gospel, so he stretches God's mercy above the bounds of His truth.

And as Satan accuses God to man, so he accuses man to God. Sometimes he does this by way of complaint, as appears in the case of Joshua (Zech. 3.1–4). In this fashion he is ever charging crimes home, and introducing bills of indictment against the saints. So that, in all his temptations, we may say, as the man said to Joab when he was asked why he had not killed Absalom: 'Thou thyself didst hear what the king commanded, that Absalom should not be hurt; and if I had done this thing, thou thyself wouldest have been the first to accuse me to the king' (2 Sam. 18.12–13). So may we answer Satan: Thou thyself dost know that God hath forbidden this thing; and if I should have done it, wouldst not thou have been the first to accuse me to God? Such is Satan's way; he is first the tempter to draw us to sin, and then an accuser to accuse us to God for sinning.

At other times Satan uses the method of suspicion and conjecture. It was so in the case of Job. God commends Job; Satan condemns him, as if he knew Job better than God Himself. Nay, and though he could not condemn Job's actions, yet he would quarrel with his affections. Surely, whatever his actions are, yet Job's intentions are not good! This was as much as to tell God that He was deceived in Job; it was as if Satan said, Certainly, whatever Thou thinkest of Job, yet Job doth not serve Thee for nought. He is a mercenary fellow, one that serves Thee for loaves, for belly blessings. Thou hast heaped outward favours on him and hast made a hedge about him, fenced him in with Thy favours so that nothing can annoy him. Thus it is that Satan brings his accusations.

But Satan cannot condemn. The issues of life and death are not in his hands, nor will his accusation against us before God take effect. A man who is himself condemned, though he has the voice of accusation, yet he has no power to condemn. His testimony against another is invalid. Satan is a condemned wretch, and all his accusations against the saints before God have no effect. Joshua's case shows this: though the accusation was true that he was clad in filthy garments, yet God would not receive it: 'The Lord rebuke thee, O Satan; is not this a brand plucked out of the fire?' (Zech. 3.2).

But it is not only Satan who accuses us; wicked men may do the same. Sometimes they do so justly, for sins committed, but forgiven, and in this they show their malice and lack of love in not forgetting that which God has forgiven. Sometimes they accuse the godly unjustly, laying to their charge things they never did, as Potiphar's wife accused Joseph of uncleanness because he would not be unclean. David, too, complains that men laid to his charge things he never did; so also, Daniel. But none can condemn the truly godly.

Again, not only Satan and wicked men, but conscience itself may accuse; and then, is it possible for us to say, Who shall lay anything to the charge of God's elect? Conscience, I say, may accuse, sometimes bringing true light, sometimes false information, sometimes reviving old bills cancelled and crossed long ago. In the first case, we are to listen to the accusations of conscience when it charges us truly. Joseph's brethren were accused by their consciences when they were evil intreated in

Egypt, and told by them that they were verily guilty of the wrong done to Joseph. After David had numbered the people, his heart smote him. Conscience had not been a bridle, and it was now a whip; it had not been a curb, therefore it was now a scourge. David did not hearken to the warnings, and therefore he feels the lashings of conscience. And when conscience justly accuses us, when it comes in with evidence according to the Word, we must hear it, for there God speaks. If a sun-dial be not set by the sun, it is no matter what it says; but if it is correct by the sun, we must hearken to it. So, if conscience does not speak according to the Word, we need not give heed to its accusations, but if it speaks according to evidence there, it is good to listen to it.

Sometimes conscience charges us falsely. It will perhaps tell us that those things are sin which are not sin. In this case it is an erroneous conscience and we are not to listen to it. At other times conscience will revive old cases, answered and satisfied long ago. Then it is a quarrelsome conscience, like a contentious troublesome fellow at law, and God will deal with it as an honest judge with such a fellow; He casts the charges out of court as matters not worth hearing, or as things that have been settled long ago. These accusations must not take hold of the soul. In this case, I say, when conscience condemns, God is greater than conscience, to acquit and absolve the soul.

But there is a fourth party which is ready to lay sin to the charge of God's people, and that is the law. The law may come as accuser. How then can it be said, 'Who shall lay anything to the charge of God's elect?', for if the law may accuse, we cannot be said to be free from the indictments and accusations of the law. I answer thus: if we speak of sins pardoned, neither conscience, nor Satan, nor law, has any right to accuse the people of God. God has justified them, and who then shall accuse?

Indeed, before faith, while we are under the law, we are subject to the accusations, judgments, and sentences of the law. The law not only accuses us then, but its sentence and curse take hold of us. It accuses us, as Christ told them that would not believe in Him, but looked for justification by the law: 'Do not think that I will accuse you to the Father: there is one that accuseth you, even Moses, in whom ye trust' (John 5.45). The law by which they looked to be justified would accuse them. The law also sentences the sinner, and the sentence and curse take hold of him: 'He that believeth not is condemned already . . . the wrath of God abideth on him' (John 3.18, 36). So that while a man is under the law, before faith and interest in Christ, the law not only accuses but also condemns him.

As for those, however, who have an interest in Christ, the law cannot accuse them of sin committed before grace saved them, because it is pardoned, and thus this accusation is made void. Nor can the law accuse them of sin after grace saved them, sin after pardon. They are not subject to the accusations, arrests, and sentences of the law. The law cannot so accuse believers as to call them into the court of the law; so the word signifies, 'Who shall lay anything to the charge of God's elect?'; or rather, Who shall call them into court? The word not only signifies to accuse, but to summon to court (*jus vocare*). Yet the believer is freed from the law as a covenant, and hence from its judgments, sentences, condemnations, curses, and accusations. If it sends any of its officers to accuse us and arrest us for sin, we may refuse to obey and to appear in its court, for we are to be tried by another court; we are to be tried by the Gospel. If God's people, when they have sinned, go to the right court, they will both sooner get sorrow for sin, and assurance of the pardon of sin; they will find more sorrow and less dismay for sin.

When I say that we are freed from the accusations of the law, I mean such accusations as are subordinate to condemnation. There is a twofold accusation, first, an accusation leading to conviction and humiliation for sin, second, an accusation

resulting in sentence and condemnation for sin. All the accusations of the law against those who are under the law come
under the second head. But all its accusations against the godly
for sin are with a view to conviction and the humiliation of
the godly under it, and so are subordinate to life and salvation. And so I conceive the law may accuse those who are,
notwithstanding, the freemen of Christ. It may show them
how far they come short of the glory of God, and how far
they have wandered from the paths of righteousness, and
may accuse them for it; but this results in humiliation, not
condemnation. As I shall show hereafter, either this must be so,
or else it must be denied that the law is a rule for believers.

But there are two queries that arise here. The first is whether
the law may justly accuse us, seeing that we are not under it.
Briefly I answer that we are not under its curses, but we are
under its commands. We are not under the law for judgment,
but we are under the law for conduct. So far as we walk not
according to it, as a rule, it has an accusing power, though we
are taken from under its condemning power. There is no
further power left in the law than is for our good, our humiliation, our edification, and this is intended to lead to our furtherance in grace.

The second query is whether the law is just in its accusations
against us, seeing we do not sin. This is founded on the previous
query; if it be true that we are freed from the law as a rule
or as a direction of life — were this so, it would be our bondage
rather than our freedom — then our breaches of the law are
not sin. If we are not subject to law, then we do not sin in
the breaking of it, any more than we do if we break the laws
of Spain or of any other nations, which are no laws to us.

I shall show later the invalidity and the danger of these two
queries. In the meantime I must tell you that the law in its
directive power remains with the believer. This must needs be
plain from the words: 'The law, which was four hundred and
thirty years after (the promise), cannot disannul (the promise),

[39]

that it should make the promise of none effect' (Gal. 3.17). For if the law, as the apostle says, was given 430 years after the promise, then it was given either as a covenant or as a rule. But as a covenant it could not be given, for then God would have acted contrary to Himself, first in giving a covenant of grace and then one of works. Therefore He gave it as a rule, to reveal to us, after our justification by the promise, a rule of walking with God so that in all things we might please Him.

Furthermore, that can never be said to be a part of our freedom which is a part of our bondage; nor can that be said to be part of our bondage which is part of our holiness. But conformity to the law, and subjection to the law of God, is part of our holiness. Therefore it can never be said to be a part of our bondage. There is, indeed, a twofold subjection – the subjection of a son, and the subjection of a slave. We are freed from the one, namely, the subjection of a slave, which was a part of our bondage, but not from the other, namely, the subjection of a son, which is a part of our freedom. But I shall speak of this at greater length in the discourses that follow.

(d) Freedom from the rigour of the law

In the fourth place, observe that the believer is freed from the rigour of the obedience required in the law. He is not freed from the requirement of exact obedience, but from that rigour of obedience which the law required as a condition of salvation.

First, the law not only commanded difficult, but also impossible things of us. It laid a yoke upon us that we could not bear, and it would not, and could not, give us the least assistance towards obedience. As it was with the scribes and Pharisees, who laid heavy yokes and burdens on men's shoulders but would not touch them with one of their fingers, so it is with the law. It lays heavy yokes upon us, but gives us not the least help or necessary strength for fulfilling its requirements. It commands, but gives neither strength nor grace for fulfilment. Therefore divines have compared the rigour of the law to the bondage of Israel under Pharaoh, who required the tale of bricks but supplied no straw. So, too, the law requires the full measure of obedience; it abates nothing in the command : but it gives no help for the fulfilment of it. It answers us in this matter as the priests did Judas, 'See thou to that'.

But now in the Gospel we are freed from impossibilities. Here all things are possible, not in respect of ourselves but in respect of God, who has undertaken to work all our works in us and for us. Chrysostom blessed God that that which God required of him, He had given to him. Indeed, the works of the Gospel are as great as any works of the law, nay, greater, namely, to believe, which is a greater work than to do all the duties of the law. But God has given us more strength; we have communion with the power and strength of Christ. Just as 'without me ye can do nothing' (John 15.5), so 'I can do all things through Christ which strengtheneth me' (Phil. 4.13). A weak Christian and a strong Christ shall be able to do all. Nothing will be too hard for that man who has the strength of Christ to enable him, and the Spirit of Christ to work with him. If God commands the works of an angel, and gives us the strength of an angel, all will be easy. The works commanded may be difficult in respect of Divine imposition, but they are easy in respect of Divine co-operation. The law was a spiritual law, but the Gospel is the law of the Spirit (Rom. 8.2). It therefore enables us to do what it commands to be done. Take one instance. In Romans 6.12, the Spirit enjoins that we should not let sin reign in our mortal bodies. That is the command. Read on in verse 14: 'Sin shall not have dominion over you, for ye are not under the law, but under grace'. There is the promise, linked with the reason for it; as if he had said, Had you been under the law you could not have expected such assistance, but you are under grace, and therefore shall have the power to obey.

Secondly, it belonged to the rigour of the law that the law required obedience in our own persons; it would not allow any to do or to work for us and help in the performance of its requirement. But we are now freed from this rigour, and God will accept of our obedience by another. There was a twofold debt that we owed to God, the debt of sin and the debt of service. These two were both transferred to Christ, and He has fulfilled all righteousness for us, both the obedience and the suffering, so that we are now said to be 'complete in him' (Col. 2.10), though in ourselves we are imperfect.

Thirdly, this belonged to the rigour of the law, that it required universal and actual, as well as personal, obedience, yea, and with such a degree of rigour that if a man failed in one tittle he was lost for ever : 'Cursed is every one that continueth not in all things which are written in the law to do them' (Gal. 3.10). Here was the call for an obedience, personal, universal, actual, constant and perpetual, failure in which in respect of any tittle at any time, brought a man under the curse of the law. All his desires, all his endeavours, would not serve the turn. If he failed in the least tittle, he was undone for ever. No repentance, no tears, no prayers, no future amends would make up for the failure. The Gospel admits of repentance, but the law will not own it. The law looks for exact obedience in every jot and tittle. From this rigid obedience has God freed the believer. Instead of universal actual obedience, God is pleased to accept of universal habitual obedience, as we find it written : 'Then shall I not be ashamed, when I have respect unto all thy commandments' (Ps. 119.6). Though there may be failing in action, yet where there is truth of affection, God can own it. In the Gospel God accepts affections for actions, endeavours for performance, desire for ability. A Christian is made up of desires, of mournings, thirstings and bewailings : O that my ways were directed! O miserable man that I am! Here is Gospel perfection.

Adam's want was will rather than power, ours rather power

than will. There is the will to do, but the lack of power to do. Not that the will is now perfect, for as we cannot do the things we would do (there is flesh in our members), so we cannot will the things we should will (there is flesh in our wills); but yet, I say, the failing of God's people is more from want of power than want of will. There is the will to do, but the power to do is lacking, as says the apostle : 'To will is present with me; but how to perform that which is good I find not' (Rom. 7.18). Yet God has mercy for 'can-nots', but none for 'will-nots'. God can distinguish between weakness and wickedness. While you are under the law, this weakness is your wickedness, a sinful weakness, and therefore God hates it. Under the Gospel He looks not upon the weakness of saints as their wickedness, and therefore He pities them. Sin makes those who are under the law the objects of God's hatred. Sin in a believer makes him the object of God's pity. Men, you know, hate poison in a toad, but pity it in a man. In the one it is their nature, in the other their disease. Sin in a wicked man is as poison in a toad; God hates it and him; it is the man's nature. But sin in a child of God is like poison in a man; God pities him. He pities the saints for sins and infirmities, but hates the wicked. It is the nature of the one, the disease of the other.

Fourthly, This again shows the rigour of the law, that it enforced itself upon the conscience with threats and with terror; but now the Gospel comes otherwise, with beseechings and with love. 'I beseech you, brethren, by the mercies of God' (Rom. 12.1). In the Gospel the spirit is not a spirit of bondage and fear, but a spirit of power and of love (Rom. 8.15; 2 Tim. 1.7). The law urges obedience upon pain of eternal death (Deut. 27.14–26; Gal. 3.10), and enforces its demands by terror, but the Gospel by sweetness and love; all terror is gone. The book of the law was placed between the cherubim and under the mercy-seat, to tell us that, under the Gospel, every law comes now to the saints from the mercy-seat.

All rigour has gone and nothing but sweetness is the motive

to it, and the principle of obedience: 'The love of Christ constrains us' (2 Cor. 5.14), as the apostle says. There is nothing more powerful than love. Things impossible to others are easy to them that love. Love knows no difficulties: 'My yoke is easy, my burden is light' (Matt. 11.30). Love is an affection that refuses to be put off by duties or difficulties which come between it and the person beloved. Jacob served a hard apprenticeship for Rachel, and yet, says the Scripture, he esteemed seven years 'but a few days, for the love he had to her' (Gen. 29.20). Love shortens time and facilitates labour. When Achilles was asked what enterprises he found the most easy of all he had undertaken in his life, he answered, 'Those which I undertook for a friend.' This is the spirit which God implants in His children, not a spirit of fear, but a spirit of love, which is the spring of all their actions, and which makes those things which otherwise would be tasks and burdens, refreshments and delights. A godly man takes in whatever concerns his happiness by faith, and lays out whatever concerns his duty by love. Faith and love are the all of a Christian. The apostle says so: 'For in Christ Jesus neither circumcision availeth anything, nor uncircumcision; but faith which worketh by love' (Gal. 5.6). Faith, like Mary, sits at the feet of Christ to hear His Word, and love, like Martha, compasses Him about with service. Faith is the great receiver, and love is the great disburser; we take in all by faith and lay out all by love. This, then, is another privilege which believers enjoy; they are freed from the rigour of the law. And there are other privileges also which, because I would hasten on, I shall but name.

(iv) Freedom from obedience to men

In the next place we observe that the believer is not only freed from Satan, from sin, and from the law; he is also freed from obedience to men. We have no lords over us; men are our brethren; and our Lord and Master is in heaven. We find in

Scripture a double charge: do not usurp mastership, do not undergo servitude. Consider the first, not to usurp mastership. We read in the Word: 'Be not ye called Rabbi: for one is your Master, even Christ; and all ye are brethren. . . . Neither be ye called masters: for one is your Master, even Christ' (Matt. 23.8–10).

As for the second, not to undergo servitude, we read: 'Ye are bought with a price; be not ye the servants of men' (1 Cor. 7.23). The meaning is, that we are not to acknowledge any our supreme master, nor are we to give our faith and consciences, nor enthral our judgments, to the sentences, definitions, or determinations of any man or men upon earth, because this would be to make men masters of our faith, which the apostle so much abhorred: 'We are not masters of your faith, but helpers of your joy' (2 Cor. 1.24). There are two kinds of masters, masters according to the flesh, and masters according to the spirit. The first kind you read of in Eph. 6.5–7: 'Servants, be obedient to them that are your masters according to the flesh'. The second kind we read of in Matt. 23.8–10, as already mentioned. To our masters according to the flesh we are to be obedient, so far as appertains to the outward man, in all outward things. But of our souls and consciences, as we have no fathers, so we have no masters upon earth, only our Master and Father which is in Heaven; and in this sense Christ speaks, that we must not absolutely yield up ourselves to be ruled by the will of any, nor enthral our judgments, nor submit our faith and consciences to any power below Christ. It were high usurpation for any to require it; it is to trespass on Christ's Royal Prerogative, and it were no less iniquity for us to render it. Thus much, then, for the fourth branch of our freedom; I may speak more upon it later.

(v) Freedom from death

Again, the believer is freed from death. There are three kinds of death: firstly, a spiritual death, the death of the soul in the body; secondly, a natural death, the death of the body from the soul; thirdly, an eternal death, the death of soul and body for ever. The first and third of these believers do not doubt of; all the question is about the second, namely, natural death, of which I shall say no more than this, that it is the body only that dies, man's inferior part, yet our dust and bones are still united to the Son of God. But the believer is freed from death as a curse. The nature of death is taken away, and therefore the name is changed. It is but called a sleep, and a sleep in Christ, and a gathering to our fathers, a change, a departing. Death is the godly man's wish, the wicked man's fear. Aristippus, being asked in a storm why he did not fear as well as others, answered: 'There is a great difference between us; they fear the torments due to a bad life; I expect the rewards due to a good life.' There is another aspect to a believer's freedom from death – he will not die until the best time. Indeed, none shall die until God's time. What David said to his enemies, so may any man say: 'My times are in thy hand' (Ps. 31.15). But this is not always the best time: you may die with Belshazzar, carousing; with Ananias and Sapphira, lying; with the nobleman, unbelieving;[1] with Julian,[2] blaspheming. But this is the privilege of saints, that they shall not die until the best time, not until when, if they were but rightly informed, they would desire to die.

Men cut down weeds at any time, but their corn they will not cut down till the best time. 'You are God's husbandry', says the apostle; you are His wheat, and when you are ripe, when you have done your work, then, and not till then, shall you be gathered into your Master's garner.

(vi) *Freedom from the grave*

Lastly, believers will be freed from the grave, and this belongs to their consummated freedom. We shall but touch the subject

[1] The reference seems to be to 2 Kings 7. 19–20.
[2] Roman Emperor (at Constantinople), 361–3; known to history as 'Julian the Apostate'.

by giving you three conclusions: (1) Though our bodies die and are consumed to dust, yet they shall rise fresh, heavenly and glorious. They shall arise perfect bodies, freed from sickness and all imperfections; spiritual bodies (1 Cor. 15.44), not in regard to substance but in regard to qualities; immortal bodies, never to die more; glorious bodies, every one filled with brightness and splendour, shining as the sun in the firmament (Dan. 12.3; Matt. 13.43). (2) The bodies rise as the same bodies. The same soul shall be re-united to the same individual body. This is a mystery. The philosophers dreamed of a transformation of bodies, or bodies transformed into new shapes; and of a transmigration of souls, or souls flitting into new bodies; but they could never apprehend the truth of this, the resurrection of the body. It was beyond them to think that this same individual and numerical[1] body should rise again after being corrupted in water, consumed by fire, converted into earth, dissipated into air, eaten up by fishes and those fishes eaten by men. When Paul disputed this point at Athens, the great philosophers of the Epicureans laughed at him: 'What will this babbler say?' But the Scripture tells us that we shall see Him with these same eyes (Job 19.27). And it agrees with God's justice that the same bodies which have sinned or suffered shall be punished or rewarded. (3) The soul and body shall never be parted more to all eternity. When a believer dies, by death he is freed from death; after this reunion there shall never be separation more.

FREEDOM IN ITS POSITIVE ASPECTS

So far, I have spoken of the negative aspects of Christian freedom.

I shall next speak a little on the positive aspect of the subject, what we are free unto, and will but name a few particulars:

[1] Numerical = identical.

(1) We are freed from a state of wrath and brought to a state of mercy and favour (Eph. 2.1–10).

(2) We are freed from a state of condemnation and brought to a state of justification (Rom. 8.1). Before, we were under the condemnation of the law because we had sinned, and of the Gospel because we believed not. But now there is 'no condemnation', not one condemnation. The law cannot condemn us because we have appealed from it; the Gospel cannot because we are now believers. God condemned sin in Christ that He might justify the sinner by Christ, and cast out condemnation for ever. 'He will bring forth judgment unto victory' (Matt. 12.10). 'He will cast out condemnation for ever' is the way in which an old writer construes the passage, and this sense it will bear.

(3) We are freed from a state of enmity and brought into a state of friendship: 'And you that were sometime alienated and enemies in your mind by wicked works yet now hath he reconciled' (Col. 1.21).

(4) We are freed from a state of death and brought to a state of life: 'You hath he quickened, who were dead in trespasses and sins' (Eph. 2.1).

(5) We are freed from a state of sin and brought into a state of service: 'We being delivered out of the hand of our enemies might serve him without fear' (Luke 1.74). For this reason God discharged the debt of sin that we might render Him the debt of service. He freed us from the bonds of misery that we might take upon us the engagements of duty (Rom. 8.12). After mentioning all the benefits brought to the believer by Christ, he draws this inference: 'Therefore, brethren, we are debtors'. He that thinks not service to be his freedom thinks not sin to be his bondage, and therefore he is in bondage.

(6) We are freed from a state of bondage, a spirit of slavery in service, and brought into a spirit of sonship and

liberty in service. As Christ by His blood redeemed us from being slaves, so by His obedience and Spirit He has redeemed us to be sons. Now we are drawn to service, not with cords of fear, but with the bands of love; not by compulsions of conscience, but by the desires of nature (2 Peter 1.4). As the love of God to us was the spring of all His actions to us, so our love to God is the source of all our obedience to Him.

(7) In a word—for we cannot stay to name all—we are freed from death and hell, and brought to life and glory. Heaven is our portion, our inheritance, our mansion house. It was made for us, and we for it; we are vessels prepared for glory (Rom. 9.23). And this is called 'the glorious liberty of the sons of God' (Rom. 8.21; Eph. 1.14). To tell you what you are freed from, and what you shall enjoy hereafter—to take you to the top of Nebo and show you all this Canaan—would make you willing to lay down your bodies there (as did Moses) and go up to enjoy it. But it is far beyond man's power to open this privilege to view, even a little. 'Eye hath not seen, nor ear heard, neither have entered into the heart of man, the things which God hath prepared for them that love him' (1 Cor. 2.9). Yet this is spoken of grace, and therefore what is glory? Could we but open this up to you, it were even enough to put you into Heaven while you are here upon earth. It is called the New Jerusalem, glory, joy, the Master's joy, the Father's house, the Kingdom of glory, Heaven, Light, Life, Eternal Life. Look but on that one place (2 Cor. 4.17): 'For our light affliction, which is but for a moment, worketh for us a far more exceeding and eternal weight of glory': glory, weight of glory, exceeding weight of glory, more exceeding weight of glory; a far more exceeding weight of glory, nay, a far more exceeding and eternal weight of glory! And this is the

glorious liberty of the sons of God! But I must conclude on this matter, because I would not willingly keep you off from that which is to be the chief part of my discourse.

We have thus briefly, as far as the breadth and scope of the subject would allow, finished the three general points which we proposed in the handling of this doctrine—the quality, the nature, and the branches of Christian freedom. I must now come to the application of what I have said, and the largeness of the subject will afford much comfort and caution, much direction and encouragement to the people of God. But I have other work to do first.

2

THE MORAL LAW A RULE OF OBEDIENCE

QUERY I : *Are Christians freed from the moral law as a rule of obedience?*

Our text (John 8.36) is the main basis whereon this doctrine of Christian freedom is built. But many have endeavoured to build their own superstructures, hay and stubble, upon it, which the foundation will never bear. Indeed, there are so many opinions which plead patronage from this doctrine that I conceive it is my great work to vindicate so excellent a doctrine as this is — true Christian freedom — from those false, and I may say licentious, doctrines which are fastened and fathered upon it. I must show you that neither this doctrine, nor yet this text, will afford countenance to, or contribute any strength to the positions and opinions which some would seem to deduce from it and build upon it.

The work is great, for I am to deal with the greatest knots in the practical part of divinity, and men's judgments are various. Scripture is pleaded on all hands. The more difficult the work, the more need of your prayers, that the Father of lights would go before us, and by His own light lead and guide us into the ways of all truth. In this confidence we shall venture to launch into these deeps, and begin the examination and trial of those doctrines which are deduced from, and would seem to be built upon, this text. The first doctrine, and the main one, that they would seem to build upon this text is, that believers are freed from the law. And this shall be the first question we will examine.

In answer to this query as it is propounded, we must confess that we are not without some places of Scripture which declare the law to be abrogated, nor without some again that speak of it as yet in force. We will give you a taste of some of them; and shall begin with those that seem to speak of the abrogation of the law.

Jeremiah 31.31–33 : 'Behold, the days come, saith the Lord, that I will make a new covenant with the house of Israel, and with the house of Judah; not according to the covenant that I made with their fathers in the day that I took them by the hand to bring them out of the land of Egypt; which my covenant they brake, although I was an husband unto them, saith the Lord: but this shall be the covenant that I will make with the house of Israel; After those days, saith the Lord, I will put my law in their inward parts, and write it in their hearts; and will be their God, and they shall be my people.'

Romans 7.1–3 : 'Know ye not, brethren (for I speak to them that know the law), how that the law hath dominion over a man as long as he liveth? For the woman which hath an husband is bound by the law to her husband so long as he liveth; but if the husband be dead, she is loosed from the law of her husband. So then if, while her husband liveth, she be married to another man, she shall be called an adulteress: but if her husband be dead, she is free from that law; so that she is no adulteress, though she be married to another man.'

That the apostle here speaks of the moral law is evident from the seventh verse; and that believers are freed from it, see the sixth verse and others. See also Rom. 6.14: 'For sin shall not have dominion over you: for ye are not under the law, but under grace'; Gal. 3.19, 'The law was added because of transgressions, till the seed should come'; Gal. 4.4–5, 'God sent forth his Son, made of a woman, made under the law, to redeem them that were under the law, that we might receive the adoption of sons'; Rom. 8.2, "For the law of the Spirit of life in Christ Jesus hath made me free from the law of sin and death'; Gal. 5.18, 'But if ye be led of the Spirit, ye are not under the law'; Rom. 10.4, 'For Christ is the end of the law for righteousness to every one that believeth'; 1 Tim. 1.8–10, 'The law is good if a man use it lawfully, knowing this, that the law is not made for a righteous man', etc.

There seems therefore to be a great deal of strength in the Scripture to prove the abrogation of the law, that we are dead to the law, freed from the law, no more under the law. These Scriptures we shall have to deal with afterwards. For the present, I only quote them, to let it be seen with what strength the Scriptures seem to hold out for the first opinion, that is, for the abrogation of the law.

On the other hand, there are some Scriptures which seem to hold up the law, and which say that the law is still in force: I say, some which seem to support the obligation, as the others the abrogation, of it. Thus there is Rom. 3.31 : 'Do we then make void the law through faith? God forbid : yea, we establish the law.' This seems contrary to the former; the verses previously given seem to speak of the abrogation, this of the establishment, the obligation, of the law. So also Matt. 5.17–18 : 'Think not that I am come to destroy the law or the prophets; I am not come to destroy but to fulfil. For verily I say unto you, Till heaven and earth pass, one jot or one tittle shall in no wise pass from the law, till all be fulfilled.' Upon these varieties of texts, men have grounded their varieties of opinions for the abrogation of, or the obligation of, the law. There is no question but the Scripture speaks truth in both; they are the words of truth; and though they seem here to be as the accusers of Christ, never a one speaking like the other, yet if we are able to find out the meaning, we shall find them like Nathan and Bathsheba, both speaking the same things.

In order to find out the truth under these seeming contraries, and for the purpose of answering the query, lest we should beat the air and spend ourselves to no purpose, it will be necessary to make two inquiries: (1) what is meant by the word 'law'? (2) in what sense is the word used in Scripture? When this has been done there will be a way opened for the clearing of the truth and for the answering of the queries.

THE SCRIPTURAL USES OF THE WORD 'LAW'

(1) What is meant by the word 'law'? I answer: the word which is frequently used for 'the law' in the Old Testament is 'Torah'. This is derived from another word which signifies 'to throw darts', and comes to signify 'to teach, to instruct, to admonish'; hence it is used for any doctrine or instruction which teaches, informs, or directs us: as, for example, in Proverbs 13.14: 'The law of the wise is a fountain of life, to depart from the snares of death.' Here 'law' is taken in a large sense for any doctrine or direction which proceeds from the wise; so, too, in Proverbs 3.1 and 4.2.

In the New Testament the word 'law' is derived from another word which signifies 'to distribute', because the law distributes, or renders to God and man their dues.

In brief, this word 'law', in its natural signification both in the Old and New Testaments, signifies any doctrine, instruction, law, ordinance, or statute, divine or human, which teaches, directs, commands, or binds men to any duty which they owe to God or man. So much, then, for the first matter.

(2) In what senses is this word 'law' used in Scripture? I shall not trouble the reader with all the uses of the word, but shall confine myself to the chief of them:

(i) It is sometimes taken for the Scriptures of the Old Testament, the books of Moses, the Psalms, and the Prophets. So the Jews understood it in John 12.34: 'We have heard out of the law that Christ abideth for ever'. So also in John 15.25: 'This cometh to pass, that the word might be fulfilled that is written in their law, They hated me without a cause' (Ps. 35.19). Similarly, we have 1 Cor. 14.21: 'In the law it is written', where the apostle is repeating the words of Isaiah 28.11, and he says they are written in the law.

(ii) The term 'law' is sometimes used as meaning the whole Word of God, its promises and precepts, as in Ps. 19.7: 'The law of the Lord is perfect, converting the soul'. Conversion is the fruit of the promise. Neither justification nor sanctification is the fruit of the law alone. The law commands but gives no grace, so that here the psalmist includes the promise of grace in his use of 'law'; or else conversion, as he speaks of it here, does not mean regeneration.

(iii) 'Law' is sometimes taken for the five books of Moses, as in Gal. 3.21: 'If there had been a law given which could have given life, verily righteousness should have been by the law'. Likewise, in John 1.45: 'We have found him of whom Moses in the law . . . did write'. Similarly in Luke 24.44: 'All things must be fulfilled which were written in the law of Moses', meaning the five books of Moses; see also Gal. 4.21.

(iv) 'Law' is used for the pedagogy of Moses, as in John 5.46: 'Had ye believed Moses, ye would have believed me: for he wrote of me.' See also Josh. 1.7–8.

(v) Sometimes 'law' is used for the moral law alone, the Decalogue, as in Rom. 7.7, 14 and 21.

(vi) Sometimes 'law' refers to the ceremonial law, as in Luke 16.16.

(vii) Sometimes 'law' refers to all the laws, moral, ceremonial, and judicial, as in John 1.17: 'The law was given by Moses, but grace and truth came by Jesus Christ': 'grace' in opposition to the moral law, 'truth' in opposition to the ceremonial law which was but a shadow. Thus Chrysostom comments on this passage: 'The ceremonial law was given right up to the time of the coming of the seed promised to Abraham.'

Among all these different usages, the controversy lies in the last-mentioned, where the word 'law' signifies the moral, judicial, and ceremonial law. In respect of two of these varieties of law, we find considerable agreement; the main difficulty concerns the moral law.

The ceremonial law was an appendix to the first table of the moral law. It was an ordinance containing precepts of worship for the Jews when they were in their infancy, and was intended to keep them under hope, to preserve them from will-worship, and to be a wall of separation between them and the Gentiles. This law, all agree, is abrogated both in truth and in fact.

As for the judicial law, which was an appendix to the second table, it was an ordinance containing precepts concerning the government of the people in things civil, and it served three purposes: it gave the people a rule of common and public equity, it distinguished them from other peoples, and it gave them a type of the government of Christ. That part of the judicial law which was typical of Christ's government has ceased, but that part which is of common and general equity remains still in force. It is a common maxim: those judgments which are common and natural are moral and perpetual.

However, in respect of the ceremonial and the judicial law we find few dissenters. All the controversy arises from the third part, the moral law.

And so we come to speak of the moral law which is scattered throughout the whole Bible, and summed up in the Decalogue. For substance, it contains such things as are good and holy, and agreeable to the will of God, being the image of the divine will, a beam of His holiness, the sum of which is love to God and love to man.

It is one of the great disputes in these days, whether this moral law is abrogated, or, in the words of the query, whether believers are freed from the moral law. All agree that we are freed from the curses and maledictions, from the indictments and accusations, from the compellings and irritations, and other particulars which we named before. But the question is, to put it in plain terms: Are believers freed from obedience to the moral law, that is, from the moral law as a rule of obedience?

Some there are who positively or peremptorily affirm that we are freed from the law as a rule, and are not, since Christ came, tied to the obedience of it. Others say that it still remains in force as a rule of obedience, though abolished in other respects, as Beza says: 'Christ fulfilled the law for us, but not in order to render it of no value to us.' We are still under the conduct and commands of the law, say these Christians, though not under its curses and penalties.

Again, others say that we are freed from the law, as given by Moses, and are only tied to the obedience of it, as it is given in Christ: and though, they say, we are subject to those commands and that law which Moses gave, yet not as he gave it, but as Christ renews it, and as it comes out of His hand and from His authority: 'A new commandment I give unto you, that ye love one another' (John 13.34). It is a commandment, for Christ is both a Saviour and a Lord; and it is a new one, not that it did not exist before, but because now renewed, and because we have it immediately from the hands of Christ.

I shall not much quarrel with this. Acknowledge the moral law as a rule of obedience and Christian walking, and there will be no falling out, whether you take it as promulgated by Moses, or as handed to you and renewed by Christ.

Indeed, the law, as it is considered as a rule, can no more be abolished or changed than the nature of good and evil can be abolished and changed. The substance of the law is the sum of doctrine concerning piety towards God, charity towards our neighbours, temperance and sobriety towards ourselves. And for the substance of it, it is moral and eternal, and cannot be abrogated. We grant that the circumstances under which the moral law was originally given were temporary and changeable, and we have now nothing to do with the promulgator, Moses, nor with the place where it was given, Mount Sinai, nor with the time when it was given, fifty days after the people came out of Egypt, nor yet as it was written in tables of stone, delivered with thunderings and lightnings. We look not to Sinai, the hill of bondage, but to Sion, the mountain of grace. We take the law as the image of the will of God which we desire to obey, but from which we do not expect life and favour, neither do we fear death and rigour. This, I conceive, is the concurrent opinion of all divines. For believers, the law is abrogated in respect of its power to justify or condemn; but it remains full of force to direct us in our lives. It condemns sin in the faithful, though it cannot condemn the faithful for sin. Says Zanchius: 'The observance of the law is necessary for a Christian man, and it is not possible to separate such observance from faith.' And as Calvin says: 'Let us put far from us the ungodly notion that the law is not to be our rule, for it is our changeless rule of life.' The moral law, by its teaching, admonishing, chiding, and reproving, prepares us for every good work. The law is void in respect of its power to condemn us, but it still has power to direct us; we are not under its curse, but yet under its commands.

Again, the moral law is perpetual and immutable. This is an everlasting truth, that the creature is bound to worship and obey his Creator, and so much the more bound as he has received the greater benefits. If we claim to be free from obedience, we make ourselves the servants of sin. But these matters I shall speak more largely upon in the discourse that follows.

Therefore, against that opinion which holds forth the abrogation of the law, and says that we are freed from obedience to it, I shall state and endeavour to make good two propositions which will serve fully to answer the query, and to refute the false notions. The propositions are these:

(1) That the law, for the substance of it (for we speak not of the circumstances and accessories of it), remains as a rule of walking to the people of God.

(2) That there was no end or use for which the law was originally given but is consistent with grace, and serviceable to the advancement of the covenant of grace.

If these two propositions are made good, the doctrines of the abrogation of the law and of freedom from the law will both fall to the ground.

PROPOSITION I: THE LAW REMAINS AS A RULE OF WALKING FOR THE PEOPLE OF GOD

We shall begin with the first proposition, namely, that the law, in the substance of it, remains in force as a rule of walking to the people of God. I shall not need to stay long over this, for when the second proposition is made good it will be seen that it establishes this also. By the law is meant the moral law comprehended in the Decalogue or ten commandments. By the substance of it, I mean the things commanded or forbidden which are morally good or evil, and cannot be changed or abolished. For what is the law in the substance of it but that law of nature engraven in the heart of man in innocency? and what was that but the express idea or representation of God's own image, even a beam of His own holiness, which cannot be changed or abolished any more than the nature of good and evil can be changed? And that the law thus considered remains as an unchangeable rule of walking to believers I am now to prove.

THE TESTIMONY OF THE REFORMED CONFESSIONS

For this proof, not to mention individuals whose testimony might be produced, even as many almost as men, we have a cloud of witnesses if we look upon the Confessions of Christian and Reformed Churches in their agreement together. The Helvetian (Swiss) Church has this confession: 'Thus far is the law of God abrogated, in that it has no power to condemn believers. . . . Notwithstanding, we do not disdainfully reject the law, but condemn them as heresies which are taught against the law, that it is not a rule of walking.' The French Church has this: 'We believe all the figures of the law to be taken away by the coming of Christ, although the truth and substance of them continue to us in Him, and are fulfilled to us in Him. But the doctrine of the law is used in them both to confirm our life and that we may be the more established in the promises of the Gospel.' Agreeable to this is the Belgic Confession.

The Wittenberg Confession includes this: 'We acknowledge the law of God, whose abridgment is in the Decalogue, to command the best, the most just and perfect works, and we hold that man is bound to obey the moral precepts of the Decalogue. Neither are those precepts which are contained in the apostles' writings a new law, but are branches of the old law.' And again, 'It is needful to teach men that they must not only obey the law, but also how this obedience pleases God.'

The Scottish Church confesses: 'We do not think we are so freed by liberty as if we owed no obedience to the law; we confess the contrary.' The Church of England holds a similar doctrine: 'Although the law given of God to Moses in regard of the rites and ceremonies does not bind Christians, neither is any, although a Christian, loosed from the obedience of the commandments which are called moral.' To these testimonies might be added many more.

But it may be that some men regard these Confessions as of no authority and therefore they have no power with them. And indeed, if these things are not proved from the Word of God, they have no power with us. We respect good men and their writings, but we must not build our faith upon them as a sure foundation. This is against our Christian liberty; we cannot be enslaved to the judgments of any. 'To the law and to the testimony; if they speak not according to this word, it is because there is no light in them.' We shall therefore give some proofs out of the Word itself, and then draw arguments from them.

THE TESTIMONY OF THE NEW TESTAMENT

We read in Matt. 5.17-18: 'Think not that I am come to destroy the law or the prophets: I am not come to destroy but to fulfil; for verily I say unto you, Till heaven and earth pass, one jot or one tittle shall in no wise pass from the law, till all be fulfilled.' This seems to be very full and very plain for the continuance of and obligation to the law. And yet there are corrupt readings of these words, and as sinister interpretations. Some would have it to be understood that Christ would not abolish the law until He had fulfilled it. Indeed, He was 'the end of the law', as the apostle speaks in Rom. 10.4, but we must understand this to mean 'the perfecting and consummating end', not 'the destroying and abolishing end' of the law. In Christ the law had an end of perfection and consummation, not of destruction and abolition. It is to be noted that in this verse Christ gives a stricter exposition of the law, and vindicates it from the corrupt glosses of the Pharisees, which surely speaks the continuance, not the abrogation, of the law. And agreeable to this is the language of the apostle in Rom. 3.31: 'Do we then make void the law through faith? God forbid: yea, we establish the law.' How? Not for justification, for in this respect faith makes it void, but as a rule of obedience, and in this respect faith establishes it. Further, the apostle tells us 'that the law is holy, just and good' and that 'he delighted in the law of God after the inward man' and also that 'with the mind I myself serve the law of God' (Rom. 7.12, 22, 25). With this agrees James 2.8: 'If ye fulfil the royal law according to the scripture . . . ye do well'. What law this was, he shows in the eleventh verse to be the Decalogue or moral law. Likewise: 'He that saith I know him, and keepeth not his commandments, is a liar' (1 John 2.4); also: 'Sin is the transgression of the law' (1 John 3.4).

Therefore, since Christ, who is the best expounder of the law, so largely strengthens and confirms the law (witness the Sermon on the Mount, and also Mark 10.19); since faith does not supplant, but strengthens the law; since the apostle so often presses and urges the duties commanded in the law; since Paul acknowledges that he served the law of God in his mind, and that he was under the law to Christ (1 Cor. 9.21); I may rightly conclude that the law, for the substance of it, still remains a rule of life to the people of God.

But I would add further arguments, beginning with this: If ever the law was a rule of walking, then it is still a rule of walking: this is clear. Either it is still such a rule, or we must shew the time when, as such, it was abrogated. But no such time can be shewed. If it is said that it was abrogated in the time of the Gospel by Christ and His apostles, we reply that no such thing can be proved. It was not so abrogated at that time. If Christ and His apostles commanded the same things which the law required, and forbade and condemned the same things which the law forbade and condemned, then they did not abrogate it but strengthened and confirmed it. And this is what they did: see Matt. 5.19: 'He that breaketh one of the least of these commandments, and teacheth men so, shall be called the least in the kingdom of heaven; but he that shall teach and observe them shall be called (not legal preachers, but) great in the kingdom of heaven.'

Therefore, in that Christ Himself expounded and established the law, by His word and authority, as shown in the fifth, sixth, and seventh chapters of Matthew, it shows us the continuance of it; for had it been His will utterly to abolish it, He would rather have declared against it, or have suffered it to die of itself; and would not have vindicated it, and restored it to its purity from the glosses of the Pharisees. All this clearly speaks to us of the continuance of, and obligation to, the law.

As with Christ, so with the apostles: instead of abolishing, in their doctrine they establish it, frequently urging the duties of the law upon the churches and people of God: 'Dearly beloved, avenge not yourselves' (Rom. 12.19). Why? 'For it is written, Vengeance is mine'. Likewise, in Rom. 13.8–10. There the apostle repeats the commandments of the second table, not to repeal or reverse any of them, but to confirm them as a rule of walking for the saints. He comprehends them all in this: 'Thou shalt love thy neighbour as thyself, for love is the fulfilling of the law.' As Beza writes: 'Love is not perfected except as the fulfilling of the law.' See also 1 Thess. 4.3, 4, 7: 'This is the will of God . . . that ye should abstain from fornication . . . that no man go beyond and defraud his brother in any matter; because that the Lord is the avenger of all such.' See also Eph. 6.1: 'Children, obey your parents in the Lord.' The apostle here presses this duty from the authority of the precept, and persuades to it from the graciousness of the promise, 'for this is the first commandment with promise' – a conditional promise (as Beza says), as are all such promises as are found in the law. As full and plain are the words of the apostle in Rom. 3.31: 'Do we abrogate the law? No, we establish it by faith.' Though it carries another sense, it bears this sense also, that though we disown the law in respect of justification, yet we establish it as a rule of Christian living.

Again, in Matt. 3.10 we read: 'The axe is laid to the root of the tree; every tree which bringeth not forth good fruit, is hewn down and cast into the fire'; and in Matt. 5.22: 'Whosoever shall say to his brother, Thou fool, shall be in danger of hell fire.' In these and sundry other places, so some learned and holy divines tell us, the comminations and threatenings of the New Testament are not of the nature of the Gospel, but are confirmation of the law, and plainly demonstrate to us the continuance of the law under grace. Thus Daniel Chamier[1] distinguishes in the Gospel between the doctrine of the Gospel and the grace of the Gospel, between the preaching of the Gospel by Christ and the apostles and the law of faith or spirit of life in Christ. The preaching or doctrine of the Gospel, he tells us, contains two things, first the promise of grace, and second, the confirmation of the law. And he shows that all those comminations and threats which we read in the Scriptures of the New Testament in no way belong to the nature of the Gospel properly so called, but are the confirmation of the law, and declare the continuation of it now under the Gospel as an exact rule to direct Christians in their walk and obedience.

FIVE PROOFS OF THE BINDING NATURE OF THE LAW

Before I proceed to the rest of the arguments, I will mention what objectors say to this. Some of them say that, though the law is a rule, yet it is a rule which we are free to obey or not to obey: it is not a binding rule. There are various opinions about this. Some say that it binds us no further than as we are creatures. I answer: if so, why then are they not bound? I hope they are creatures as well as Christians. Others say that it binds the flesh but not the spirit; it binds the unregenerate part, but not the regenerate part of a man, to obedience, for the regenerate part is free. I answer: here is a dangerous gap, open to all licentiousness; witness the opinions of David George[2] and the Valentinians.[3] Others say that the law is not a binding rule at all and that believers are no more under the law than England is under the laws of Spain; that Christians

---

[1] Chamier (1565–1621) served various Reformed congregations in France. He was killed by a cannon-ball during the siege of Montauban.

[2] David George (d. 1556), otherwise David Joris, was a religious fanatic in the Netherlands and Germany. He formed a sect in which he was virtually regarded as a messiah. He taught that 'a man filled with the Spirit is sinless, no matter what deeds he may commit'.

[3] Valentinians: a second-century sect founded by the gnostic, Valentinus. It claimed that a Christian was 'law-less'.

are no more bound to the obedience of the law than men are bound to the obedience of the laws of another commonwealth than their own; to speak otherwise, they say, overthrows Christian liberty.

Now if this be true, it strikes down all. If it be a rule, but not a binding rule, a rule binding to obedience, it will be of small use. We will end this cavil, therefore, before we go any further, and show that the law is indeed a binding rule, and that it binds Christians, not as men, but as Christians. I will give five arguments in proof of this:

(1) That which being observed, causes the consciences of regenerate men to excuse them, and which, not being observed, causes their consciences to accuse them, is binding on the conscience. But it is the law of God which thus causes the consciences of the regenerate to excuse or else to accuse them. Therefore the law of God is that which is binding on the Christian conscience.

(2) That which has power to say to the conscience of the regenerate Christian, This ought to be done, and that ought not to be done, is binding on the conscience. But the law of God has this power. Therefore, though it cannot say that this or that ought not to be done on pain of damnation, or on pain of the curse; or this or that ought to be done in reference to justification or the meriting of life; yet it shows it ought to be done as good and pleasing to God, and that this or that ought not to be done, as things displeasing to Him.

(3) The authority by which the apostles urged Christians to duty binds the conscience to obedience. But the apostles used the authority of the law to provoke Christians to their duty (as in Eph. 6.1–2). Therefore the law is the rule by which Christians must walk.

(4) If the law of God does not bind the conscience of a regenerate man to obedience, then whatever he does which is commanded in the law, he does more than his duty; and so either merits or sins, being guilty of will-worship. But in

obedience to the law he is not guilty of will-worship, neither does he merit: 'When ye have done all those things which are commanded you, say, We are unprofitable servants; we have done that which was our duty to do' (Luke 17.10).

(5) Either the law binds the conscience of Christians to obedience, or Christians do not sin in the breach of the law. But they sin in the breach of it, as says 1 John 3.4: 'Sin is the transgression of the law'. Therefore, the transgression of the law is sin. Or look at it thus: If Christians are bound not to sin, then they are bound to keep the law. But Christians are bound not to sin; therefore they are bound to keep the law. I know that objectors will agree that Christians are bound not to sin, but that they will deny that they are bound to obey the law; but I will prove my point in this way: If he that breaks the law sins, then Christians are bound to keep the law if they are not to sin. But he that breaks the law does sin, as says the apostle: 'Sin is the transgression of the law' (1 John 3.4), and 'Where no law is there is no transgression' (Rom. 4.15). Therefore Christians are bound, if they would avoid sin, to obey the law.

And now, being driven against the wall, the objectors have no way to maintain the former error but by another. They tell us plainly that believers do not sin: 'Be in Christ and sin if you can.' But the apostle tells them that they sin in saying this: 'If we say that we have no sin, we deceive ourselves, and the truth is not in us' (1 John 1.8). Nay, we 'make him (that is, God) a liar' (v. 10). 'If we say', includes the apostles as well as others, for 'there is no man who sins not' (1 Kings 8.46). 'In many things we offend all' (James 3.2).

FIVE FURTHER ARGUMENTS FOR OBEDIENCE TO THE LAW

But if this will not silence them, then they say that God sees no sin in those who are believers. But what is this? It is one thing to sin, and another for God not to see sin. Indeed, He sees not sin, either to condemn believers for sin, or to approve and allow of sin in believers. He sees not sin, that is, He will not see sin to impute it to us when we are in Christ. But if this does not convince the objectors, then they say: Though believers sin, and though God sees it, for He sees all and brings all into judgment, yet God is not displeased with the sins of believers. I reply:

1. Certainly, perfect good must for ever hate that which is perfect evil, and the nearer it is to Him, the more God hates it. In a wicked man, God hates both sin and sinner, but in a believer, He hates the sin, though He pities and loves the poor sinner. He is displeased with sin, though He pardons sin through Christ. But we will follow this no longer. Thus much must suffice for the proof and vindication of the first argument.

2. If the same sins are condemned and forbidden after Christ came as were forbidden before He came, then the law, in respect of its being a rule of obedience, is still in force; but the same sins are thus condemned and forbidden. That which was sin then is sin now. I speak of sin against the moral law. Therefore the moral law is still in force to believers as their rule of obedience.

3. If the same duties which were enjoined in the law are commanded believers under the Gospel, then the law still remains as a rule of direction and obedience. But the same duties are commanded under the Gospel as were enjoined under the law, as I have already shown (e.g. Rom. 13.9–10 and Eph. 6.1). Therefore the law still remains as a rule of obedience under the Gospel.

4. If the things commanded in the law are part of holiness and conformity to God, and if this conformity to the law is required of us, then we conclude that the law is still in force. But the things commanded are part of Christian holiness, and conformity to the law is required of us. Therefore the law is still in force. That the things commanded are part of our holi-

ness, I suppose is granted. If so, that this conformity to the law is required of us, it is easy to prove. That which we are to aspire to, and labour for, and after which we are to endeavour both in our affections and actions, in our principles and practices, that, surely, is required of us. But this is all the same with conformity to the law of God. That we are to aspire to such conformity in our affections is clear from Rom. 7.22, 25, where the apostle shows us that he delighted in the law of God, and that he served the law in his mind. Nay, it was his purpose, aim, desire, and endeavour of heart, to be made conformable to that law which he says is 'holy, just, and good'. Though he fell short of it, yet he aspired after it; which shows we too are to aspire after it in our affections. And it is equally plain that we are to endeavour after conformity to it in our actions. Take both together: 'Thou hast commanded us to keep thy precepts diligently. O that my ways were directed to keep thy statutes! Then shall I not be ashamed, when I have respect unto all thy commandments' (Ps. 119.4–6). He has respect to them in his heart and affections; and he seeks conformity to them in life and actions. And this was his duty, because God had commanded: 'Thou hast commanded us to keep thy precepts. O that my ways were directed to keep thy statutes!'

5. It cannot be part of our freedom by Christ to be freed from obedience to the law, because the law is holy, just, and good. Surely it is no part of our freedom to be freed from that which is holy, just, and good! Consider it in this way: That cannot be part of our freedom which is no part of our bondage. But obedience and subjection to the moral law in the sense I have showed was never part of our bondage. Therefore to be freed from obedience to the law cannot be part of our freedom. I will prove that it was never part of our bondage.

That cannot be part of our bondage which is part of our glory; but obedience and conformity to the law, both in principle and in practice, is part of our glory; therefore it cannot be part of our bondage. Again, that cannot be said to be part of our bondage which is part of our freedom. But to obey the law is part of our freedom, as we read in Luke 1.74: 'That we, being delivered out of the hand of our enemies, might serve him without fear, in holiness and righteousness before him, all the days of our life.' I shall proceed no further upon this. It is plain enough, that the law in the substance of it remains a rule of walking or obedience to them in Christ. We shall give two or three applications and then come to the second matter.

(i) *Application against Papists*

The foregoing will serve to show the error of the Papists in their unjust charge against us that we make it a part of our Christian liberty to be exempted from all law and to live as we list, and that we are not bound to the obedience of any law in conscience before God. We appeal to all the Reformed Churches in the Christian world, whether ever any of them did put forth such an opinion as this. It is the concurrent opinion of all Reformed Churches that Christians are subject to the rule, the direction, and the authority of the moral law, as says Chamier: 'Believers are free from the curses, not from the obligations, of the law.' We preach obedience to the law, but not as the Papists do. They preach obedience as a means to justification; we preach justification as a means to obedience. We cry down works in opposition to grace in justification, and we cry up obedience as the fruits of grace in sanctification. He that does not walk in obedience is a stranger yet to Christ; and he that rests in his obedience does not know Christ. Indeed, many are too much like the Jews still. God set up a law as a rule of walking, and they look for justification by it. These poor men are like oxen in the yoke; they draw and toil and spend their strength (for who do more than those who think to earn merit thereby?), and when they have performed their labour, they are fatted up for slaughter. So it is with these: when they have endeavoured hard after their own righteousness, they perish in their just condemnation. These men Luther fitly calls 'the devil's martyrs': they suffer much, and take much pains to go to hell. The apostle tells them what they are to expect: 'For as many as are of the works of the law are under the curse' (Gal. 3.10), that is, those who are under the works of the law for justification; and the apostle gives the reason, 'for it is written, Cursed is every one that continueth not in all things which are written in the book of the law to do them'. These men seek life in death, righteousness in sin. And, alas, we are all too apt to follow this line; it is hard to perform all righteousness and rest in none; hard to be in duties in respect of performance, and out of duties in respect of dependence. We are apt to weave a web of righteousness of our own, to spin a thread of our own by which we may climb up to heaven. Were it not so, what is the need for so many exhortations and admonitions to perform all righteousness but to rest in none? The Scripture does not make a practice of killing flies with beetles,[1] or cleaving straws with wedges of iron; nor does it spend many admonitions and exhortations where there is no need.

Alas, there are multitudes in the world who make a Christ of their own works, and this is their undoing. They look for righteousness and acceptance more in the precept than in the promise, in the law rather than in the Gospel, more in working than in believing; and so they miscarry. There is something of this spirit in us all; otherwise we should not be up and down so much in respect of our comforts and our faith, as is still so often the case. We become cast down with every weakness in ourselves. But we should be *all* in Christ in weak performance, and *nothing* in ourselves in strong performances.

(ii) *Against Antinomians*

We look next at the case of those who are called Antinomians.[2]

---

[1] A long-handled, heavy-headed hammer.
[2] The term may have been coined by Luther, but its use in England appears to date from 1644. Literally, it means 'against law', and was used to describe professing Christians who claimed that the moral law was not binding upon them. Hence with many it came to signify a person holding loose moral standards, a loose-liver.

Just as the Papists set up the law for justification, so the Anti-nomians decry the law for sanctification. We claim to be free from the curses of the law; they would have us free from the guidance, from the commands of the law. We say we are free from the penalties, but they would abolish the precepts of the law. They tell us that we make a false mixture together of Christ and Moses, and that we mingle law and Gospel together. How unjustly they lay this charge against us, let men of under-standing judge. We cry down the law in respect of justifica-tion, but we set it up as a rule of sanctification. The law sends us to the Gospel that we may be justified; and the Gospel sends us to the law again to inquire what is our duty as those who are justified. Whatever they say of the law, though they cast contempt and disgrace upon it, and upon those who preach it, yet we know that, for the substance of it, it is the image of God, a beam of His holiness. The things therein commanded and forbidden are things morally, and therefore eternally, good and evil; nothing can alter the nature of them. Things not by nature either good or evil are alterable by him that commanded them. But those things which are morally good or evil, God can no more alter them than make evil good, or good evil. That which was morally good formerly is morally good now, and is to be pursued and practised. That which was for-merly morally evil is morally evil now, and is to be shunned and avoided. We have a Gospel rule which turns us to obedi-ence to the law. We find it in Phil. 4.8 : 'Whatsoever things are true, whatsoever things are honest, whatsoever things are just, whatsover things are pure, whatsoever things are lovely, whatsoever things are of good report; if there be any virtue, and if there be any praise, think on these things.' And I hope the law is of this number. The apostle tells us that the law is 'holy and just and good'; certainly in it there is nothing com-manded but what is good. If we are to learn of the ant, and from brute beasts, certainly are we much more to learn from the law, which is the image of God in man and the will of God to man. We have nothing to do with Moses, nor do we look to Sinai, the hill of bondage, but we look to Zion, the mountain of grace. We take the law as the eternal rule of God's will, and we desire to conform ourselves to it, and to breathe out with David, 'O that my ways were directed to keep thy statutes!' Certainly the law and the Gospel help one another; they lend one another the hand, as says Peter Martyr.

The law is subservient to the Gospel. Its purpose is to convince and humble us, and the Gospel is to enable us to fulfil the obedience of the law. The law sends us to the Gospel for our justification; the Gospel sends us to the law to frame our way of life. Our obedience to the law is nothing else but the expression of our thankfulness to God who has freely justified us, that 'being redeemed, we might serve Him without fear' (Luke 1.74). Though our service is not the motive or impelling cause of God's redeeming of us, yet it is the purpose of our redemption. The apostle shows this at length in the sixth chapter of Romans; it is the application he makes of the doctrine of free justification. He continues: 'Therefore, brethren, we are debtors' (Rom. 8.12). If Christ has freed us from the penalties, how ought we to subject ourselves to the precepts! If He has delivered us from the curses, how ought we to study the commands! If He paid our debt of sin, certainly we owe a debt of service.

This was the great end of our redemption; He redeemed us from bondage and brought us into freedom, from slavery to service. That which Christ has redeemed us *to*, He cannot be said to redeem us *from*; but He has redeemed us unto service, and therefore cannot be said to redeem us from service. Indeed, He has freed us from the *manner* of our obedience, but not from the *matter* of our obedience. We now obey, but it is from other principles, by other strength, unto other ends, than we did before.

Previously, the principles of obedience were legal and servile, now they are filial and evangelical. As the law was given with evangelical purposes, so it is now kept from evangelical principles, principles of faith, love, and delight, which causes the soul to obey, and facilitates the whole of obedience. The love of Christ constrains (2 Cor. 5.14), yet is the obedience free. Love knows no difficulties; things impossible to others are easy to them that love. The grounds of obedience differ: heretofore, fear, now love. Previously the strength was our own; now we have fellowship with the strength of Christ. Our works are said to be wrought in God, by union with Him (John 3.21), and by fellowship with Him. As we can do nothing without Him, so we can do all things through Christ who strengthens us. And this strength He has promised: 'The Lord hath avouched thee this day to be his peculiar people, as he hath promised thee, and that thou shouldest keep all his commandments' (Deut. 26.18). He tells us that He works all our works in us and for us (Isa. 26.12), the required works of grace in us, and of duty for us.

The ends before were for justification and life; now they are for other ends – to glorify God, to dignify the Gospel, to declare our sincerity, to express our thankfulness. Before, we obeyed, but out of compulsion of conscience; now we obey out of the promptings of nature, which, so far as it works, works to God, as naturally as stones move downward or sparks fly upward. Thus, then, it is that we preach the law, not in opposition to, but in subordination to the Gospel, as we shall show at length later.

(iii) *To all believers*

Lastly, under this head, let me exhort you all to judge of the law aright, and then let it be your care to maintain it. Let not Moses take the place of Christ; but, at the same time, make a right use of Moses. When works and obedience take their right place, when the law is rightly used, then it is holy, just and good. But if we use it as our life, then we trample the blood of Christ underfoot, and make His life and death in vain. Let the servant follow the Master; let Moses follow

Christ; the law, grace; obedience, faith; and then all act their proper and designed parts. Remember what Zacharias said: 'You were redeemed that you might serve' (Luke 1.74), that you might live unto Him that died for you. Reason from mercy to duty, not from mercy to liberty. O beware that the great things of Christ do not make you more careless! Take heed not to abuse mercy. It is a sad thing when Christians abuse the grace of Christ. The justice of God prevails with others; oh, but God would have His tender mercies prevail with you: 'I beseech you therefore, brethren, by the mercies of God, that ye present your bodies a living sacrifice' (Rom. 12.1). The reasonings of saints are to be from engagements of mercy to enlargements in duty (2 Cor. 5.14 and 7.1). Having such precious promises, let us purge ourselves from all corruptions of the flesh and spirit. None but venomous spirits will, spider-like, suck poison from such sweets, or draw such inferences from mercy as may be encouragements to sin.

It would be a sad matter if believers should grow more slack and sluggish; if that which should quicken them slackens their hands; if a man should say in his heart, Christ died, I need not pray so much; Christ has done all, therefore I need do nothing. The doctrine we advance should strengthen and not weaken your engagement to duty, should heighten and not lessen your engagement to duty; it should quicken and not deaden your hearts' affections; it should inflame and not cool your spirits.

Worse still would it be if we should draw arguments to sin from mercy received. Should that become a spur which should be the greatest curb? 'Shall we sin because grace abounds?' (Rom. 6.1). 'There is mercy with thee, that thou mayest be feared', says the Psalmist (130.4), not that I may sin, but that I may serve. You whom the law has sent to the Gospel, let the Gospel again send you to the law; study now your duty; abundance of mercy calls for abundance of duty. If God had not abounded in mercy, what would have become of us? And has

He abounded in mercy? Oh, then, let us abound in duty; let us obey for God's sake who gives us His Son; for Christ's sake who has given Himself that we might give ourselves to God; for faith's sake which is dead without obedience. It is the cry of faith, Give me children, else I die. Obey for the sake of your profession of His Name. Adorn the Gospel of our Lord and Saviour Jesus Christ. What a shame if it should be said of us that faith cannot do that which unbelief is able to do! What will Turks and Mohammedans say – 'Look, these are the people who reverence Christ! These are the servants of the crucified God! They profess Christ and yet will forswear and will sin against Christ!' What will Papists say? 'These are they who preach faith, and yet are strangers to obedience, and live in sin.'

No, let the righteousness of the law be fulfilled in us; let us walk not after the flesh, but after the Spirit' (Rom. 8.4). The law is a royal law: 'If ye fulfil the royal law according to the scripture', says James, 'ye do well' (2.8). It is a royal law, that we might live royally above the ordinary rank of men in obedience. 'Receive not the grace of God in vain' (2 Cor. 6.1). If you receive it not in vain, you will have power to will, and power to do; you will prize grace and walk thankfully. It was wittily spoken by one – and there is some truth in the saying – 'Live as though there were no Gospel; die as though there were no law. Pass the time of this life in the wilderness of this world under the conduct of Moses; but let none but Joshua bring you over into Canaan, the promised land.'

The saying agrees thus far with Scripture. Moses was a man of the law; he gave the law and he is often taken as representing the law: 'They have Moses and the prophets' (Luke 16.29); 'There is one that accuseth you, even Moses, in whom ye trust' (John 5.45). Joshua was a type of Christ; his name signifies so much; he was Jesus, so called in Heb. 4.8: 'If Jesus', that is, Joshua, 'could have given them rest'. Moses must lead the children of Israel through the wilderness, but Joshua must bring them into Canaan. So while you are in the wilderness of this world, you must walk under the conduct of Moses; you must live in obedience to the law. But it is not Moses but Joshua, not works but faith, not obedience but Christ, who must bring you into Canaan. Do what you can while you live; but be sure to die resting on Christ's merits.

This must suffice under our first main proposition; that the substance of the law is a rule of obedience to the people of God, and that to which they are to conform their lives and their walk now under the Gospel. This we have proved by the Scriptures, by a cloud of witnesses, by the concordant testimony of the Reformed Churches. We have strengthened this by many arguments, and given some applications of the doctrine.

3

LAW AND GRACE

PROPOSITION 2: THE LAW IS NOT INCOMPATIBLE WITH GRACE

The next part of our first main query will prove more knotty than the first, but if we are able to make it good, it will at once vindicate the law, and overthrow the many erroneous opinions that are in conflict with it. Our proposition is that there was no end or use for which the law was given which was incompatible with grace and which was not serviceable to the advancement of the covenant of grace. This I hope to make good, and then it will be seen how the Gospel is in the law; also that the law is not that which some men make it out to be, that is, opposite to the Gospel and to grace; for I shall show that it may run along with grace, and be serviceable to the advancement of grace.

In the prosecution of this matter we shall follow this method:

(1) We shall first explain the chief and principal ends for which the law was promulgated or given;

(2) We shall explain how those ends are consistent with grace and serviceable to the advancement of the covenant of grace; and therefore that they may continue under grace;

(3) We shall answer such objections as may be raised against this doctrine;

(4) We shall sum up the matter in few words and make a brief application.

First of all, then, my work is to show the chief and principal ends for which the law was promulgated or given. There are two main ends to be observed, one was political, the other theological or divine. The political use is hinted at by the apostle in 1 Tim. 1.8–9: 'Knowing this, that the law is not made for a righteous man, but for the lawless and disobedient, for the ungodly and for sinners, for unholy and profane, for murderers of fathers and murderers of mothers, for manslayers', etc; that is, it was made for them in such fashion that, if it were not their rule, it should be their punishment. Such is the political use of the law.

Its second great purpose was divine, or theological; and this is two-fold, as seen in those who are not justified, and as seen in those who are justified. In those who are not justified, the law first reveals their sin to them, humbles them for sin, and so drives them to Christ. In those who are justified it acts first of all as a doctrine to drive them to duty, next as a glass to reveal their defects so that they may be kept humble and may fly to Christ, next as a restrainer and corrector of sin, and then again as a reprover of sin (2 Tim. 3.16).

I must, however, state the principal and chief ends for which the law was promulgated:

(1) To restrain transgression; to set bounds and banks to the cursed nature of fallen man, not only by revealing sin, but also the wrath of God against sin: 'tribulation and anguish to every soul of man that doeth evil' (Rom. 2.8–9). We read in Gal. 3.19 that 'the law was added because of transgressions'. This Scripture Jerome and Chrysostom understand to refer to the restraining of transgressions. The law may restrain sinners,

though it cannot renew sinners; it may hold in and bridle sin, though it cannot heal and cure it. Before God gave the law, sin had a more perfect reign. By reason of the darkness of men's understandings, and the security of their hearts (Rom. 5.13–14), death reigned, and so sin, from Adam to Moses, as the apostle shows. Therefore God might give them the law to show them, not only that they sinned in such courses as they walked in, but to show them also that heavy wrath of God which they drew upon themselves by their sin, the effect of which might be to restrain them in their course of sin, and to hinder sin so that it could not now have so complete and uncontrolled a dominion and reign in the soul. Though it continued to reign – for restraining grace does not conquer sin, though it suppresses and keeps it down – yet it could not have full dominion. The sinners would be in fear, and that would serve to restrain them in their ways of sin, though not to renew them.

If God had not given a severe and terrible law against sin, such is the vileness of men's spirits, they would have acted all villainy. The Devil would not only have reigned, but raged in all the sons of men. And therefore, as we do with wild beasts, wolves, lions, and others, binding them in chains that they may be kept from doing the mischief which their inclinations carry them to, so the law chains up the wickedness of the hearts of men, that they dare not fulfil those lustful inclinations which are found in their hearts.

Blessed be God that there is this fear upon the spirits of wicked men; otherwise we could not well live in the world. One man would be a devil to another. Every man would be a Cain to his brother, an Amnon to his sister, an Absalom to his father, a Saul to himself, a Judas to his master; for what one man does, all men would do, were it not for a restraint upon their spirits. Naturally, sin is oblivious to sense and shame too. There would be no stay, no bank, no bounds to sin, without the law. Therefore we have cause to bless God that he has given a law to restrain transgression, that if men will not be so good as they should be, yet, being restrained, they become not so bad as they would be. Were it not for this, and for the awe that God has cast upon the spirits of wicked men by means of it, there would be no safety.

The fields, the streets, your houses, your beds, would have been filled with blood, uncleanness, murder, rapes, incests, adulteries, and all manner of mischief. If there were no law, saying, 'Thou shalt do no murder', men would make every rising of passion a stab. If there were no law saying, 'Thou shalt not steal', men would think theft, deception, cheating, and oppression good policy, and the best life would be 'ex rapto vivere' (living by robbery), living by other men's sweat. If there were no law saying, 'Thou shalt not commit adultery', men would defile their neighbour's bed, and commit all manner of wickedness.

For these reasons God has given a law to set bounds and banks to defend us against the incursions and breaches that sin would make upon us. He that sets bounds and banks to the raging sea, which otherwise would overflow the land, also sets bounds and banks to men's sins and sinful affections. It is no less wonder that the deluge of lust and corruption in men does not break forth to the overflowing of all banks, than that the sea does not break forth upon us, but He that sets bounds to the one, also binds and restrains the other. This, then, is one purpose God has in giving the law.

(2) Secondly, the law was given to uncover and reveal transgression, and this, I conceive, is the true meaning of the apostle's words in Gal. 3.19: 'The law was added because of transgressions', that is, chiefly, that the law might be 'instar speculi' (like a glass) to reveal and discover sin. Therefore says the apostle: 'Is the law sin? God forbid. Nay, I had not known sin, but by the law: for I had not known lust, except the law had said, Thou shalt not covet' (Rom. 7.7). The apostle seems to say the same thing in Rom. 5.20: 'The law entered that the offence might abound', that is, that sin might appear exceed-

ingly sinful. And this is another end God had in giving the law, to open, to reveal, to convince the soul of sin. And this was with reference to the promise of grace and mercy.

It was for this reason God gave the law after the promise, to reveal sin and to awaken the conscience, and to drive men out of themselves, and bring them over to Christ. Before He gave the law, men were secure and careless. They did not esteem the promise and the salvation which the promise offered. They did not see the necessity for it. Therefore God gave the law to discover sin, and by that to reveal our need of the promise, that in this way the promise and grace might be advanced. In giving the law, God did but pursue the purpose of mercy He had in giving the promise, by taking a course to make His Gospel worthy of all acceptation, that when we were convinced of sin, we might look out for and prize a Saviour; when we were stung by the fiery serpent, we might look up to the brazen serpent – in all this, I say, God was but pursuing the design of His own grace.

(3) Thirdly, the law was given to humble men for sin, and this is a fruit of the former, as we have it in Rom. 3.19–20: 'Now we know that what things soever the law saith, it saith to them who are under the law : that every mouth may be stopped, and all the world become guilty before God', that is, sensible of their own guilt. We were no less guilty before, but now by the law men are made sensible of their own guilt, for, says the apostle, 'By the law is the knowledge of sin'. It is also written, 'Where there is no law, there is no transgression' (Rom. 4.15), that is to say, no transgression appears where there is no law to discover it, or no transgression is charged upon the conscience where there is no law to discover sin. This seems to be excellently set out in Rom. 5.13–14: 'Until the law sin was in the world, but sin is not imputed when there is no law. Nevertheless death reigned from Adam to Moses', etc. The meaning is, there was no less sin, or guilt and death, before the law than after; sin reigned, and death reigned

over all the sons of men, and it reigned the more because it reigned in the dark; there was no law given by which sin was discovered and revealed to them, and to help to charge sin upon them. And so the apostle says, 'Sin is not imputed when there is no law', that is, though sin and death did reign, yet men were secure and careless, and having no law to discover sin to them, they did not charge their own hearts with sin; they did not impute sin to themselves. Therefore God renewed the law, promulgating it from Sinai, to discover and impute sin to men, to charge them with sin. I will explain the matter by means of a similitude.

Suppose a debtor to owe a great sum of money to a creditor, and the creditor out of mere mercy promises to forgive him all the debt, yet afterwards sends forth officers to arrest and lay hold of him; it would be concluded that the man was acting contrary to himself and had repented of his former promises, when actually he had not changed at all and had repented of nothing, his only desire being that his mercy might be the more conspicuous and evident in the thoughts of the debtor; therefore he allows him to be brought to these extremities that he may become the more thankful. The case is the same between God and us. We are deeply indebted to God. To Abraham, and to us in him, God made a promise of mercy, but men were careless and secure, and though they were guilty of sin, and therefore liable to death, yet, being without a law to evidence sin and death to their consciences, they could not see the greatness of the mercy which granted them a pardon. Thereupon God published by Moses a severe and terrible law, to reveal sin, to accuse men of sin, and to condemn men for sin. Not that God intended that the sentence should take hold of the sinner, for then God would be acting contrary to Himself, but in order that thereby guilt might be made evident, men's mouths stopped, and that they might fall down and acknowledge the greatness and riches of free grace and mercy. Thus it was in Job, as is shown fully in Job 33.16–31. And again: 'The Scripture hath concluded all under sin, that the promise by faith of Jesus Christ might be given to them that believe' (Gal. 3.22).

(4) The law was given for a direction of life, a rule of walking to believers. This I showed at large formerly: that though the law as a burden to the conscience is removed, yet it is not removed for purposes of obedience. If it were needful, I might pursue this matter further, to strengthen believers. The moral law is certainly perpetual and immutable. It is an everlasting truth that the creature is bound to worship and obey his Creator, and so much the more bound as he has received great benefits. This is a truth which is as clear as the light, and, surely, to be free from obedience is to be servants unto sin, as already showed.

(5) The law was given, not only as a director of duties, but as a glass to reveal the imperfections in our performance of duties, that so we might be kept humble and vile in our own eyes, and that we might live more out of ourselves and more in Christ. It was given so that we might fly to Christ upon all occasions, as a defiled man flees to the fountain to be washed and cleansed, for in Christ there is mercy to cover, and grace to cure all our infirmities.

(6) The law was also given as a reprover and corrector for sin, even to the saints; I say, to discipline them, and to reprove them for sin. 'All Scripture . . . is profitable for doctrine and reproof' (2 Tim. 3.16), and this part of Scripture especially for these ends, to be 'instar verberis' (like a scourge), to correct and chastise wantonness, and correct a believer for sin. As says Calvin: 'The law by teaching, warning, admonishing, correcting, prepares us for every good work.'

(7) The law was given to be a spur to quicken us to duties. The flesh is sluggish, and the law is 'instar stimuli' (of the nature of a spur or goad) to quicken us in the ways of obedience. Thus much, then, for the ends for which the law was given.

I am next to show that there was no end for which the law was given which was incompatible with grace and which might not be serviceable to the covenant of grace; therefore the law may remain in force to be serviceable under grace.

1. The law was given to restrain transgressions, and it is of the same use now. It restrains wicked men from sin, though it has no power to renew and thus change them. Fear may restrain, though it cannot renew men. Fear may suppress sin, though faith alone conquers and overcomes sin. The law may chain up the wolf, but it is the Gospel that changes the wolfish nature; the one stops the streams, the other heals the fountain; the one restrains the practices, the other renews the principles. And who does not see that this is the ordinary fruit of the law of God now? It was the speech of a holy man that Cain, in our days, has not killed his brother Abel; that our Amnon has not defiled his sister Tamar, that our Reuben has not gone up to his father's couch; that our Absalom has not conspired the death of his father. It is because God restrains them. For this reason was the law added, and for this purpose it continues, to restrain wicked men, to set bounds and banks to the rage of men's lustful hearts.

2. Secondly, the law was given to discover and reveal transgressions, and this is not inconsistent with grace; nay, it serves to advance it, and it still continues for this end, even to discover and reveal transgressions in believers, to make sin and misery appear, and by that means to awaken the conscience to fly to Christ. Hence the apostle says: 'Wherefore then serveth the law? It was added because of transgressions, till the seed should come to whom the promise was made' (Gal. 3.19). Some take 'seed' here to mean the saints of God, and make this the meaning, that so long as there are any to be brought to Christ, so long will there be the use of the law to reveal sin both in

the unregenerate, that they may fly to Christ, and in the renewed, that they may learn to direct all their faith, hope, and expectation on Christ still. Whether this interpretation holds good or not, yet this is firm truth, that the law remains with us for this purpose, to reveal sin to us. 'Where no law is, there is no transgression' (Rom. 4.15), that is, no sin is discovered; where there is no law to perform this work, sin does not appear. But 'the law entered that the offence might abound' (Rom. 5.20), not only to bring sin to light, but to make it appear exceedingly sinful. The words of the apostle put this beyond all question, 'I had not known sin but by the law' (Rom. 7.7). The law was the revealer of sin to him. He says in verse 13: 'But sin, that it might appear sin, working death in me by that which is good; that sin by the commandment might become exceeding sinful.'

It is clear, therefore, that the law still retains this use; it discovers sin in us. 'I had not known lust, except the law had said, Thou shalt not covet' (Rom. 7.7); and similarly with all sins. This it does, after grace has come, as well as before grace; that which was sin before is sin now; grace does not alter the nature of sin, though it does set the believer free from the fruits and condemnation of it.

3. Thirdly, the law was added to humble us for sin. This also agrees with grace, and its usefulness in this respect still remains, though some would deny it. Sin is the great reason for humiliation, and that which is a glass to discover sin, must needs upon the discovery of it, humble the soul for it. In respect of this, read Rom. 3.19–20 and Gal. 3.22. In this regard it may be said that the law is not against the promises of God (Gal. 3.21), 'but the Scripture hath concluded all under sin, that the promise by faith of Jesus Christ might be given to them that believe'. The apostle says that the law is not against the promises. The affirmative interrogations which he employs are the strongest negations. And he shows why the law is not against the promise, because it is subservient to the promise.

'The law serves the cause of the Gospel', says Chamier, 'because, convicting men of their works of condemnation, it prepares them to seek the grace which is found in the Gospel.'

The law concludes men under sin; it humbles them, convinces them of sin, that so the promise might be given. Hence it is said in Gal. 3.24: 'Wherefore the law was our schoolmaster to bring us unto Christ, that we might be justified by faith.' He speaks of the same law as is mentioned earlier in the chapter, which seems (by verse 22) to be the moral law. And how is this the schoolmaster, but by lashing us, humbling us for sin, and driving us to Christ? Or if it is argued that it was the ceremonial law which is meant by the schoolmaster, yet the moral law was the rod. The master does little without the rod, nor the ceremonial law without the moral law. It is the moral law which drives men to the ceremonial law, which was in former days Christ in figure, as it does now drive us to Christ in truth.

Thus the law remains, an instrument in the hand of the Spirit, to discover sin to us, and to humble us for it, that so we might come over to Christ. If the avenger of blood had not followed the murderer, he would never have gone to the city of refuge, and if God does not humble us we would never go to Christ. An offer of Christ and of pardon before men are humbled is unavailing. Men do by this as those did who were invited to the supper; they made light of it. Just so, men make light of a pardon, and of the blood of Christ. But when once God has discovered sin to them; when the law has come to them, as it came to Paul, with an accusing, convincing, humbling, killing power, Oh then, Christ is precious, the promise is precious, the blood of Christ is precious. I conceive that this was the main end for which God gave the law after the promise, to cause sinners to value the promise. Men would not have known the sweetness of Christ if they had not first tasted of the bitterness of sin.

4. Fourthly, the law was given for a direction of life, and so it does still remain and serve, as I have already fully proved. Though we are sons, and are willing to obey, yet we must learn how to direct this willing disposition. I say, though we are sons and are guided by the Spirit, and though in our love to God we are ready for all service, yet we need the Word of God to be a light unto our feet and a lantern to our paths. God has made us sons and he has given us an inheritance; and now He gives us a rule to walk by, that we may express our thankfulness to Him for His rich mercy. Our obedience is not the cause and ground of His act of adoption, but the expression of our thankfulness and of the duty we owe to God who has adopted us. God therefore did not give the rule, and afterwards the promise; but first the promise, and then the rule, to show that our obedience was not the ground of our acceptance, but a declaration of our gratitude to the God who has accepted us. Thus it remains our rule of walking, yet in Christ. It must be our rule in Christ; we must obey by the strength of Christ. Obedience begins from Christ, not that we work for an interest in Christ, but we get such an interest that we may work.

The law, say some of our divines, was given with evangelical purposes, that is, with purposes subservient to the Gospel. And I say it must be obeyed from evangelical principles, principles rooted in Christ. The law shows us what is good, but gives us no power to do it. It is 'lex spiritualis' (a spiritual law), holy, just and good; but it is not 'lex spiritus' (the law of the spirit); this is alone in Christ, as the apostle speaks in Rom. 8.2: 'The law of the Spirit of life in Christ Jesus'. The law shows us what is holy, but cannot make us holy, as long as it is a rule outside of us. It cannot make us holy, for that necessitates a rule within us.

The law is a principle within us first, and then a pattern without us. We are not made holy by imitation, but by implantation. But that principle found within sends us to the law as to the rule without, after which we are to conform our lives

[87]

without. When the law is once our principle, it then becomes our pattern.

5. Fifthly, the law was given us as a glass to reveal our imperfections in duty, and for this purpose the law remains with us. Through it we perceive the imperfections of our duties, our graces, and our obedience. By this means we are kept close to Christ and kept humble. The law takes us away from reliance on ourselves and casts us upon Christ and the promises.

Thus have we seen God's purposes and ends in introducing the law; we have also seen how these ends are not only consistent with grace, but also serviceable to the advancement of the work of grace. We come next to objections which may be raised against this doctrine, and when I have answered these I shall leave this first and main query after some application of the same.

Objections answered : (1) *That the law as a covenant is incompatible with grace*

The first objection I shall deal with is this : that the law was set up as a covenant, and if so, it was in contrast with grace and incompatible with grace.

That it was introduced and set up as a covenant, certain passages of Scripture seem to declare, as, for example, Exod. 19.5 : 'Now therefore, if ye will obey my voice indeed, and keep my covenant, then ye shall be a peculiar treasure unto me above all people.' Still more plainly does it appear in Deut. 4.13 : 'And he declared unto you his covenant, which he commanded you to perform, even ten commandments; and he wrote them upon two tables of stone.' And again – Jer. 31.31-33 : 'Behold, the days come, saith the Lord, that I will make a new covenant with the house of Israel, and with the house of Judah : not according to the covenant that I made with their fathers in the day that I took them by the hand to bring them out of the land of Egypt; which my covenant they brake, although I was an husband unto them, saith the Lord; but this shall be the covenant that I will make with the house of Israel; After those days, saith the Lord, I will put my law in their inward parts, and write it in their hearts; and I will be their God, and they shall be my people.' So it is quoted in Heb. 8.7–9 with the explanation, 'For if that first covenant had been faultless, then should no place have been sought for the second.' These places seem to speak very plainly, that the law was given as a covenant of works to the Jews. And as a covenant of works it would not be consistent with grace, and therefore, it is argued, there were certain ends for which the law was introduced which were not consistent with grace.

For the clearing of these difficulties, let it be said that divines have distinguished between various kinds of covenants. Some of them have set down these three: a covenant of nature, a covenant of grace, a mixed kind of covenant consisting of nature and grace.

Other divines have distinguished the following:

1. 'Foedus natura', or that covenant which God made with man in innocency.
2. 'Foedus promissi', or the covenant of grace and promise, which was made with Adam after his fall in the words: 'The seed of the woman shall bruise the serpent's head', and renewed to Abraham in Genesis, chapter 15, but more clearly in Gen. 22.18: 'In thy seed shall all the nations of the earth be blessed'. So runs the covenant of grace.
3. 'Foedus operi', or the covenant of works which was made with the Jews, as they interpret the verses already quoted, Exod. 19.5 and Deut. 4.13.

Still others make the three covenants to be the following:

1. 'Foedus natura': the covenant of nature made with Adam.

[89]

2. 'Foedus gratiae': the covenant of grace made with us in Christ.
3. 'Foedus subserviens', or the subservient covenant which, they say, was the covenant made here with the Jews merely by way of subserviency to the covenant of grace in Christ, a covenant of preparation, to make way for the advancement of the covenant of grace in Christ. This, they say, as a covenant, has already gone, though the subserviency of it still remains.

Still others say that there were never more than two covenants made with man, one of works, the other of grace, the first in innocency, the other after the fall. Yet, they add, this covenant of grace was dispensed to the Jews in such a legal manner that it seems to be nothing else but the repetition of the covenant of works. In respect of this legal dispensation of it, the same covenant under the law is called a covenant of works, but under the Gospel with its clearer manifestations it is called a covenant of grace. These then, they claim, were not two distinct covenants, but one and the same covenant differently dispensed.

That the law could not be a covenant of works in the true sense of the term, is shown by the following arguments:

(1) I cannot conceive that that could be called a covenant of works under which a holy God is married to a sinful people; but by the covenant described in Jer.31–33, God was married to such ('although I was an husband unto them'). Therefore it could not be a covenant of works.

(2) That could never be said to be a covenant of works which had mercy in it to sinful men, but this covenant had such mercy. It was set up with merciful purposes, in subservience to the Gospel, as the apostle shows at length in Galatians, chapter 3.

(3) If the law was given as a covenant of works, then it would be opposite to, and contrary to, the promise; but the

apostle shows that this is not so: 'Is the law against the promises of God? God forbid' (Gal. 3.21). But if it were set up as a covenant of works, then it was diametrically opposite to it; for if salvation is of works, then is it not of grace.

(4) That can never be a covenant of works which was added to the covenant of grace; but the apostle shows that the law was added to the promise (Gal. 3.19). If it had been added as a covenant, then it would overthrow the nature of the promise. But it was so added that the nature of the promise might be preserved. But if anything of works were here, it would clean overturn grace, and overthrow the nature of the promise. Therefore it was not added as a covenant, nor was it added as an ingredient of the promise, as if justification was to come to man partly by working and partly by believing, for this would overthrow the freeness of the promise spoken of in Rom. 11.6: 'If salvation be of works, then is it no more grace'. But it was added by way of subserviency to the promise, as the apostle says: 'It was added because of transgressions'. It was so added to the promise, or covenant of grace, as to help and advance it, not subvert and destroy it. Therefore it could not be added as a covenant of works.

(5) A fifth argument may be taken from Gal. 3.17: 'The law, which was four hundred and thirty years after (the promise), cannot disannul, that it should make the promise of none effect.' But if God had introduced the law as a covenant, it would have disannulled the promise. It would also have declared God to be changeable, which cannot be, for, as the apostle says, 'God is one' (Gal. 3.20); He is the same in His grace and purpose to sinners, even though He seems, by giving the law after the promise, to repent of His former mercy, and by this means to cancel or repeal what He had done previously. Yet it is no such matter, for God is one; He is the same in all. This covenant was established by oath (Heb. 6.17–18), and when God swears, He cannot repent (Ps. 110.4). If God set this up as a covenant after He had given the promise, either this

would have showed mutability in God's will, or contradiction in His acts, which cannot be. Therefore the law could not be a covenant of works.

(6) If it were God's purpose to give life and salvation to the lost sons of men by a covenant of grace, then He never set up the law as a covenant of works for that end. But this was His purpose, as the apostle tells us in Gal. 3.18: 'If the inheritance be of the law, it is no more of promise; but God gave it to Abraham by promise.' As if he had said, It was never God's purpose to give life by the law, for He had given it before in another way, namely, by promise. Therefore it was never intended by way of law.

(7) If the law were a covenant of works, then the Jews were under a different covenant from us, and so none were saved, which the apostle gainsays: 'We believe that through the grace of the Lord Jesus Christ we shall be saved, even as they (the Gentiles)' (Acts 15.11): or else they are both under a covenant of works and a covenant of grace. But this they could not be, as they are both utterly inconsistent the one with the other.

(8) God never appoints anything to an end to which the thing appointed is unserviceable and unsuitable. But the law was utterly unserviceable and unsuitable to this end, to give life and salvation: the apostle tells us the law could not do it (Rom. 8.3). Also in Gal. 3.21: 'If there had been a law given which could have given life', which implies that it could not do it, and therefore God never introduced it for that purpose.

(9) It could never suit with God's heart to sinners to give a covenant of works after the fall; because man could do nothing; he was dead and powerless. Besides, it was contrary to the nature of a covenant; man was impotent and could not stand as a party in covenant with God.

Besides, if the nature of a covenant of works is considered, it will be seen quite plainly that it is impossible for the law to be a covenant of works:

(a) The covenant of works is a covenant between two friends. It is a covenant of friendship. But God could not make such a covenant with fallen man. We were enemies, we were guilty sinners; therefore a covenant of friendship could not be made. Indeed, there might be a covenant of grace made with man, for that is a covenant of reconciliation, and such a covenant might be made with enemies; but there could not be a covenant of works made, for that is a covenant between friends, and such we were not after the fall.

(b) The covenant of works was a covenant wherein each party had his work. It was a conditional covenant; man had something to do if he expected to receive that which was promised. But such a covenant God could not make with man after man's fall, for man could not meet the least of its terms or perform the meanest of its conditions. Therefore

(c) The covenant of works was a covenant no way capable of renewal. If man once broke it, he was undone for ever. But the covenant which God actually made with man was capable of being renewed, and men frequently renewed covenant with God. Therefore this could not be the covenant of works. Plainly, then, it was not a covenant of works which God made with the Jews.

Objection (2): *That the law is not the covenant of grace, nor a third covenant, and must therefore be a covenant of works*

But an objector may say: A covenant it was, and so it is called. If so, it is either a covenant of works, or a covenant of grace, or else 'datur tertium' (given as a third), that is, a third, or middle covenant. But there is no middle covenant, nor is it a covenant of grace; therefore it must needs be a covenant of works:

I answer: If by a third covenant is meant a middle covenant, consisting partly of works, and partly of grace, under which the Jews were placed, and by which they were saved, I utterly deny any such covenant. For there was no such covenant ever made with fallen man, neither can there be any middle course between works and grace. The apostle says plainly: 'If of works, then is it no more grace' (Rom. 11.6). If man had been required to do anything to help in the procuring of life, though never so small, and if the Gospel had provided all the rest, yet it would still have been a covenant of works, and utterly inconsistent with the covenant of grace. For, as Augustine says, 'Grace can no way be called grace, if not every way grace.' If there was anything of man's bringing, which was not of God's bestowing, though it were never so small, it would overturn the nature of grace, and make that of works which is of grace. If a man should ask but a penny of us for the purchase of a kingdom, though he should give us the rest, yet would that penny hinder it from being a mere gift and grace. So it is here. And therefore I can by no means allow a middle covenant.

There are two other opinions which I will here mention. Some men think it neither a covenant of works, nor a covenant of grace, but a third kind of covenant distinct from both. Others think it a covenant of grace, but more legally dispensed.

Those who consider it to be a third covenant speak of it as a preparatory, or a subservient covenant, a covenant that was given by way of subserviency to the covenant of grace, and for the setting forward or advancing of the covenant of grace. Those men who hold this view say that there are three distinct covenants which God made with mankind—the covenant of nature, the covenant of grace, and the subservient covenant.

The covenant of nature was that whereby God required from the creature as a creature perfect obedience to all divine commandments, with promise of a blessed life in Paradise if man obeyed, but with the threat of eternal death if he disobeyed the command, the purpose of all this being to declare how virtue pleased, and sin displeased God.

The covenant of grace was that whereby God promised pardon and forgiveness of sins and eternal life, by the blood of

Christ, to all those that should embrace Christ, and this was purposed by God to declare the riches of His mercy.

The subservient covenant, which was called the old covenant, was that whereby God required obedience from the Israelites in respect of the moral, ceremonial, and judicial laws. Blessings in the possession of Canaan were promised to obedience, and curses and miseries to those who broke the covenant, and all to this end, that God might thus encourage their hearts in the expectation of the Messiah to come.

This subservient or old covenant is that which God made with the people of Israel in Mount Sinai, to prepare them to faith, and to inflame them with the desire of the promise and of the coming of Christ; also it was meant to be as it were a bridle of restraint, and to withhold them from sin, until the time came when God would send the Spirit of adoption into their hearts, and govern them with a more free spirit.

This covenant, of which the moral law is said to be a part, and which is called here the subservient covenant (under which were the Jews), is described by the writer who propounds it, to be a third and distinct covenant, mid-way between the covenant of nature and the covenant of grace. In his treatise on the matter he states the points of difference and agreement which he sees between it and the covenants of nature and of grace. Take first the differences and agreements with the covenant of nature. The agreements are these:

1. In both these covenants (i.e. of nature and of subserviency), one party covenanting is God, the other is man.

2. Both covenants have a condition annexed to them.

3. The condition is, in general, the same—'Do this and live'.

4. The promise is, in general, the same—Paradise and Canaan.

These are the agreements. I will now show the disagreements:

1. The covenant of nature was made with all men, the subservient covenant with the Israelites alone.

2. The covenant of nature brings us to Christ, not directly by itself, but obliquely and 'per accidens' (accidentally); but the old or the subservient covenant brings us to Christ of deliberate intent and 'per se' (of itself), for this was the true and proper scope which God aimed at in the giving of it. 'God did not make the covenant of nature with man, that he, being burdened with the weight of it, should go to Christ. In giving that, God aimed at this, to have that which was His due from man. But in this subservient covenant God requires His right for no other end than that man, being convinced of his weakness and impotency, might fly to Christ.'

3. The covenant of nature was made with man, that by it men might be carried on sweetly in a course of obedience, for it was engraven on their hearts. But the subservient covenant was made that men might be compelled to yield obedience, for it did naturally beget to bondage (Gal. 4.24).

4. The covenant of nature was to be eternal, but this subservient covenant was but for a time.

5. The covenant of nature had no respect to the restraint of outward sins, neither in its principal nor lesser uses, but the old covenant in its lesser uses had this in view, as explained in Exod. 20.20.

6. The covenant of nature was engraved in the heart, but the other was written on tables of stone.

7. The covenant of nature was made with Adam in Paradise, but the subservient covenant at Mount Sinai.

8. The covenant of nature had no mediator; the subservient covenant had Moses for a mediator.

9. The one covenant was made with man perfect, the other with a part of mankind fallen.

These are stated to be the main agreements and differences between the covenant of nature and this subservient covenant. We come now to show the differences and agreements which it has with the covenant of grace : first the points of agreement: God is the Author of both, both are contracted with fallen men, both reveal sin, both bring men to Christ, both are contracted by a mediator, in both, life is promised.

Their points of difference are as follows:

1. In the subservient covenant, God is considered as condemning sin and approving only of righteousness, but in the covenant of grace He is seen as pardoning sin and renewing holiness in fallen man.

2. They differ in the stipulation or condition attached to each: that in the old covenant runs, 'Do this and live'; that in the new, 'Believe and thou shalt be saved'.

3. They differ in age. The promise was more ancient than the law. It is recorded that the law was added to the promise, and that, four hundred and thirty years after the promise was given (Gal. 3.17).

4. The subservient covenant restrains man, but by coercion and slavish restraint; but the covenant of grace works in him a willing and child-like inclination of spirit, so that obedience is free and natural.

5. In the subservient covenant, the spirit of bondage is given, but in the covenant of grace the Spirit of adoption is given.

6. The old covenant terrified the conscience; the covenant of grace comforts it.

7. The object of the old covenant was man asleep, or rather man dead in sin; of the other, man awakened, and humbled for sin.

8. The one shows the way of service but gives no strength for the service; the other both shows the way and gives the power to serve.

9. Both covenants promise life, but the one in Canaan, the other in heaven.

I have thus explained the opinion of certain divines which, though they do not seem to meet all difficulties, are nevertheless reasonable. The main reason underlying the opinion seems to be this. The law is said to be a covenant, as I have showed from various Scriptures, and if so, it is either a covenant of works, or of grace, or else a third type of covenant, neither one of works nor of grace.

It cannot be a covenant of works, as I have explained at length previously, for there was a former covenant, a covenant of grace, made, and this was but added to it, not by way of opposition to it, but by way of subserviency. Besides, this covenant, being broken, was capable of renovation, which a covenant of works is not capable of. And again, when they had broken it, they were not to think the case hopeless, but had liberty of appeal from the law to the Gospel, from God's justice offended to God's mercy pardoning and covering their sin, as we find the people frequently doing when they implored mercy and pardon for His Name's sake: 'For thy name's sake forgive, and for thy name's sake cover our transgressions'; under which expressions Christ was darkly foreshadowed.

Again, if it had been a true covenant of works, a covenant of life and death, then could they have had no mercy, no pardon, but must needs have perished. But against this the apostle speaks: 'We believe that through the grace of the Lord Jesus Christ, we shall be saved, even as they' (Acts 15.11). Nay, and then it would have been utterly inconsistent with the covenant of grace; there would have been some ends and uses for which the law was promulgated which were altogether destructive to the promise and covenant of grace. But I have already showed that there were no such ends. Therefore it must be concluded that it was such a covenant as did not stand in contradiction to the covenant of grace; therefore it could not be a covenant of works. If so, say these divines of whom I am speaking, then it must be either a covenant of grace, or some kind of third covenant.

But they say that it could not be a covenant of grace either. For our divines in general reckon this to be one part of our freedom in Christ, that we are freed from the law as a covenant, and if the law were a covenant of grace, only more legally dispensed and administered after a more legal manner, it might seem better to say that we are freed from this aspect of it rather than to say we are freed from it as a covenant. Therefore, if they say we are freed from it as a covenant, it cannot possibly be held to be the covenant of grace. This seems to be the reason underlying this opinion.

If it be neither a covenant of works, nor a covenant of grace, then must it of necessity be a third kind of covenant: and it must needs be such a covenant as does not stand in opposition to grace, nor is inconsistent with the covenant of grace, for if this be not so, then God will have contradicted Himself, overthrown His own purpose, and repented of His own promise which He had given before. Hence it is called a subservient covenant. It was given by way of subserviency to the Gospel and a fuller revelation of the covenant of grace; it was temporary, and had respect to Canaan and God's blessing there, if and as Israel obeyed. It had no relation to heaven, for that was promised by another covenant which God made before He entered upon the subservient covenant. This is the opinion which I myself desire modestly to propound, for I have not been convinced that it is injurious to holiness or disagreeable to the mind of God in Scripture.

There is, however, a second opinion in which I find that the majority of our holy and most learned divines concur, namely, that though the law is called a covenant, yet it was not a covenant of works for salvation; nor was it a third covenant of works and grace; but it was the same covenant in respect of its nature and design under which we stand under the Gospel, even the covenant of grace, though more legally dispensed to the Jews. It differed not in substance from the covenant of grace, but in degree, say some divines, in the economy and external administration of it, say others. The Jews, they agree, were under infancy, and therefore under 'a schoolmaster'. In this respect the covenant of grace under the law is called by such divines 'foedus vetus' (the old covenant), and under the Gospel 'foedus novum' (the new covenant): see Heb. 8.8. The one was called old, and the other new, not because the one was before the other by the space of four hundred and thirty years, but because the legal administrations mentioned were waxing old and decaying, and were ready to disappear and to give place to a more new and excellent administration. 'That which decayeth and waxeth old is ready to vanish away.' The one covenant was more obscurely administered, shadowed, darkened with shadows; the other was administered more perspicuously and clearly. The one was more onerous and burdensome, the other more easy and delightful. The one through the legal means of its administration gendered to bondage, the other to son-like freedom. All this may be seen clearly in Col. 2.17; Heb. 10.1; Gal. 3.1–4.3. Hence, as Alsted tells us, the new and old covenants, the covenants of the law and Gospel, are both of them really covenants of grace, only differing in their administrations. That they were virtually the same covenant is alleged in Luke 1.72–75: 'To perform the mercy promised to our fathers, and to remember his holy covenant'. What was 'his holy covenant'? It is made clear in verse 74 that in substance it was the same as the covenant of grace: 'That he would grant unto us, that we being delivered out of the hand of our enemies might serve him without fear, in holiness and righteousness before him, all the days of our life'.

For brevity's sake I will give a summary of the thoughts of those divines who maintain this second opinion. They assert:

1. There were never more than two covenants made with mankind, which held out life and salvation; the first was the covenant of works, made with man in innocency; the other is the covenant of grace, made after the fall.

2. There was but one way of salvation, one only, since the Fall, and that was by a covenant of grace; God never set up another covenant of works after the Fall; He sets us now to believe, without working for life.

3. Nevertheless, all Adam's posterity lie under the covenant of works, as Adam left them after his fall, until they come over to Jesus Christ.

4. The law was never given as a covenant of works, but added to the promise by way of subserviency to the covenant of grace.

5. Though the law was given with merciful purposes, and as subservient to the covenant of grace, yet it seems to reach man as though it were the repetition of another covenant of works under which man stands. Or rather, the covenant of grace under the Old Testament seems to be so presented as if it were still a covenant of works to man. And it is worthy of observation that the covenant of grace, like the sun in the firmament, as it rises to its zenith, becomes ever clearer. From Adam to Moses it was very dark and obscure; from Moses to the time of the prophets light began to appear. The light was clearer still when John the Baptist began his ministry. Then came the ministry of Christ Himself, when there were more clear and glorious manifestations of the covenant, for He revealed the bosom counsels of His Father. After Christ's resurrection and the sending of the Holy Spirit, the book previously clasped became fully opened, that he that runs may read. Hence some have called the covenant of grace before Christ's coming, 'foedus promissi' (the covenant of promise); and now, under the Gospel, the covenant of grace in respect of its full, clear, and ample unfolding. The shadows which obscured it in former times have been taken away, and the whole platform of God's design to save man by sheer grace is so clearly revealed that he that runs may read it.

Objection (3): That as the covenants of law and of grace are opposites, the law cannot be linked with grace

We now come to deal with the third objection raised by some, namely, that that which stood upon opposite terms to the covenant of grace cannot be described as a covenant of grace, but must needs be a covenant of works. But the law stood upon such opposite terms; therefore it must be a covenant of works. To which I answer thus:

That the law stood upon opposite terms is manifest, for in one case there is the command to do, in the other to believe: as is found, for example, in Lev. 18.4–5: 'Ye shall do my judgments and keep mine ordinances, to walk therein: I am the Lord your God. Ye shall therefore keep my statutes and my judgments: which if a man do, he shall live in them: I am the Lord.' And again in Ezek. 20.11: 'And I gave them my statutes, and shewed them my judgments, which if a man do, he shall even live in them.' And again in Gal. 3.12: 'The law is not of faith: but the man that doeth them shall live in them.'

But these passages may be thus explained. The Word does not say: 'He that doeth them shall live by them', but 'shall live in them'. We live in obedience, but we do not live by obedience. There is much difference between the two statements.

Lest this difference should be evaded, see it plainly recorded in Rom. 2.13: 'For not the hearers of the law are just before God, but the doers of the law shall be justified.' That the apostle speaks here of the moral law he shows in verses 21 and 22 where he discourses of certain branches of the moral law. Likewise in Rom. 10.5–11: 'For Moses describeth the righteousness which is of the law' (he does not say 'by the law'), 'that the man which doeth those things shall live by them. But the righteousness which is of faith speaketh on this wise . . . whosoever believeth on him shall not be ashamed.' So that the law seems to stand upon opposite terms to grace. This is the objection which is presented, and which I have shown in all its fulness. If this can be cleared, then all is done.

Now against all this I might oppose various other Scriptures which seem to speak against it, for instance, Gal. 3.11: 'But that no man is justified by the law in the sight of God, it is evident; for the just shall live by faith.' Again, Gal. 3.21: 'If there had been a law given which could have given life, verily righteousness should have been by the law.' That is, if the law had been able to justify and save any man, God would never have sent Christ. But 'by the deeds of the law there shall no flesh be justified in his sight' (Rom. 3.20; see also Ps. 143.2). 'As many as are of the works of the law are under the curse' (Gal. 3.10). If, then, all who look for life by obedience to the law are under the curse, surely God did not set up the law to the end that we should have life by obedience to it. 'The law entered that sin might abound', says the apostle, and if the law was given to show the full extent of sin, and the greatness of sin, then surely there is no possibility that man should be justified by it. Besides, it was given four hundred and thirty years after the promise. God gave the promise of life and justification previously to faith, and if afterwards He had given the law so that man might have life by working, then He would have acted contrary to Himself. He would have shown Himself changeable in His purpose, as if He repented of His former mercy. But this cannot be; therefore the other cannot be.

Besides, God could not expect men to work that they might have life, because the promise of life was given before they could do any work. Christ said, 'Without me ye can do nothing'. We have no life out of Christ; He is our life. 'He that hath the Son hath life, and he that hath not the Son hath not life.' 'That I come, however feebly, to Thee', said Chrysostom, 'is not possible except by means of Thee.' Dead men cannot work. We are incapable of working that we might live. Indeed, in Christ we are made alive that we might work.

Again, God never purposed to give life to man upon man's obedience, for He had decreed another way to confer life upon man, as may be read plainly in Gal. 3.11 where the apostle is debating this very matter: 'But that no man is justified by the law in the sight of God, it is evident.' And how is it evident? Because, says he, 'the just shall live by faith'. It is as if he had said, God has decreed another way to life, and therefore surely the former is not the way.

Yet the objector may say, It seems as if the law did require us to work, and promised us life for so doing; and if so, then certainly the law stands upon opposite terms to grace, and therefore can be neither a covenant of grace, nor subservient to it. And if they do not stand upon opposite terms, how shall we understand the Scripture, 'Do this and live?'

In answer to this objection, I will lay down six or seven particular matters for consideration:

(1) 'Do this and live' has not reference to the moral law only, but to the ceremonial law also (as in Lev. 18.4–5), which was their Gospel. This will especially appear if we look upon the ceremonial law not as an appendix to the moral law, but as it bears a typical relation to Christ, just as every lamb slain in sacrifice pointed to Christ, and said, 'Behold the lamb of God that taketh away the sin of the world'. The Gospel was darkly administered and shadowed forth in the ceremonial law.

(2) 'Do this and live' was not spoken of the law abstractly and separately considered, but of the law and the promise jointly; not of the law exclusively, but of the law inclusively, as including the promise, and as having the promise involved with it.

(3) God does not bid men, Do and live *by* doing, but Do and live *in* doing. We may live in obedience, though we do not, and cannot, live by obedience. We could not *live* by doing, till we had life; but life is not by doing, but by believing, as Christ says, 'Ye will not come to me that ye might have life'; here, clearly, it was not by works, but by grace. 'If there had been a law given that could have given life' – either life, that we might obey, or life upon our obedience – 'verily righteousness should have been by the law'.

(4) Some writers think that God, after He had given the promise of life, and tendered life upon believing, repeated the

covenant of works in the law, to put men upon the choice of being saved by working or by believing. This, they say, God did, so as to empty them of themselves, and teach them the folly of thinking that they could obtain life by obedience. Therefore God puts them to the trial; and lest they should think that any wrong was done to them, He gives them a repetition of the former covenant, and as it were gives them the choice of being saved by working, or saved by believing. Then, convinced of their own impotency, they might better see, admire, adore, and glorify the mercy of God who has given a promise, and sent a Christ, to save those who were not able to do anything towards their own salvation.

(5) Others think that 'Do this and live' has reference merely to a temporal and prosperous life in the land of Canaan. If the people would be conformable to the law which God had given them, and would obey Him in His commands, then should they live, and live prosperously, in the land of Canaan which He had given them: He would bless their basket and store, and give them many other blessings, as listed in Deuteronomy chapter 28.

(6) Another interpretation is this: that 'Do this and live', though it was spoken to the people of Israel in person, did not terminate with them, but through them was spoken to Christ, who has fulfilled all righteousness for us, and purchased life by His own obedience.

Some of these six points I reject entirely, and I cannot heartily go with any of them, but I state them to show the variety of interpretations which have been propounded. I will give briefly my own thoughts of the matter.

I grant that, viewed externally, the law and the Gospel do seem to stand upon opposite terms. But these seemingly opposite terms had, in the case of the law, ends subservient to Christ and grace. For the terms of the law were intended to awaken men, and convince them of their own impotency, to humble them for their impotency, and to drive them to Christ for salvation. If we look upon the law *separately* from the Gospel, it does seem to stand upon opposite terms. If we take it to mean that man must work for salvation and life, then certainly it is against the promises of God. But the apostle deals with this matter when he asks the question, 'Is the law against the promises of God?', to which he replies, 'God forbid.' Hence we must not look upon the law separately from the Gospel. We must look upon it *relatively*, as it has respect to the promise, and then the seemingly opposite terms of the two covenants will be seen, in the case of the law, to have ends subservient to the promise and grace. As is said by Peter Martyr: 'The law and the Gospel give us in turn their hand.' The law by showing us our helplessness causes us to go over to Christ and the promise for life. We have already seen that this was the difference between the covenant made with man in innocency and that which God required in the law. In the former, God did not require obedience so that man might become burdened with the rigour of His requirements and flee to Christ. It was simply God's aim to receive that which was His due from man. But in the law, God's sole purpose is to require His right so that man might become convinced of his weakness and helplessness, and fly to Christ. So that, although 'Do this and live' seems to be against the promise, yet if we look at the end which God had in view in giving the law, to convince man of his impotency, to humble him for it, and to drive him away from all hope in himself, then we can see a sweet agreement and subserviency of the law to the promise.

Jerome propounds a seeming contradiction, yet it is true in both of its parts: 'Cursed is he that saith, God commands impossibilities. And cursed is he that says, The law is possible.' This seems strange. Did not God command the law, and is not the law possible? It is true that it is so. But God did not command the law with the expectation that we could or should fulfil it; we were not able to obey it, nor could it help us to do so. Both of these impossibilities are seen in Rom. 8.3: the flesh was weak, therefore the law was weak. But God spoke the words, 'Do this and live', to show us our weakness and to stir up our hearts to seek Christ, who has fulfilled all righteousness for us, both positive and negative. He has undergone the penalties, and obeyed the precepts, borne our curses, and performed our services.

The course that Christ takes with the rich young ruler is very observable, and fully proves what I have been saying. It is recorded in Matt. 19.16–22: 'Good Master', says he, 'what good thing shall I do, that I may have eternal life?' Here was his question. Christ's answer is in the latter part of verse 17: 'If thou wilt enter into life, keep the commandments'. This was a strange answer. Was the law a way? If so, why had Christ come into the world? And was the young man able to keep the law? That is impossible, as Rom. 8.3 assures us; and does not the apostle say, 'As many as are of the works of the law are under the curse, for it is written, Cursed is every one that continueth not in all things which are written in the book of the law to do them.' Strange answer therefore! Christ did not say, as in other places, If thou wilt enter into life, Believe; but here, 'Keep the commandments'. Yet if we look upon the person to whom Christ spoke, and the purpose of the saying, we shall see the meaning. The person was a proud ruler, one puffed up with the proud notion that he had kept the whole law and therefore ought to have been saved by the law, as he says afterwards; 'All this have I kept from my youth up'. Therefore Christ sets him upon fulfilling the law, not as an instrument of justification (for He answers the same question otherwise in John 6.28–29), but that he may find in the law a glass to reveal to him his imperfections and impotency, and that, being humbled by it, he might seek unto Christ for life and salvation.

When men will be saviours of themselves, when they look for righteousness by the law, Christ bids them go and keep the commandments (*servanda mandata*), and this He does to humble them and to bring them to Himself. But if men are humbled and broken by a sight of their sins, then, without mention of the law at all, He comforts them with the free promises of grace, saying: 'Come unto me, all ye that labour and are heavy laden, and I will ease you', and again, 'The Spirit of the Lord is upon me to preach liberty to the captives, to set at liberty them that are bruised', and so on. 'The afflicted one', says Calvin, 'is comforted by the passing by of the law and by mention of the gracious word of promise.'

So then to conclude: I conceive the opposition between the law and the Gospel to be chiefly of man's own making. Men should have been driven to Christ by the law, but instead they expected life in obedience to it. This was their great error and mistake. It proved as hard to turn them from seeking life by their own righteousness and obedience to the law, as to force the sun from the sky. I do not think, however, that they imagined they could achieve righteousness by the moral law alone, for there they could not help but see that it was an impossibility, but they hoped to obtain it by joining the ceremonial law with the moral. God had given them these laws, and had often said, 'Do this and live'. Therefore they hoped by subjection to them to have life. And what they lacked in the moral, they tried to make up in the ceremonial; they would do something of what the moral law commanded, and go to the ceremonial law for what they could not do. Not that all did this, yet many of them did so.

But this was far from God's purpose. It was their own error and mistake, as the apostle seems to imply in Rom. 10.3–4: 'They have a zeal of God, but not according to knowledge. For they being ignorant of God's righteousness, and going about to establish their own righteousness, have not submitted themselves unto the righteousness of God.' They went about it, but could not attain it. All this was but setting a dead man on his feet; and this arose from their ignorance, their error and mistake. They did as poor ignorant souls do with us; we bid them pray, we bid them obey and perform duties; and, poor souls, all they do, they do with the idea that they can thereby justify themselves. They spin a thread of their own righteousness in which to apparel themselves. Poor souls, they can think of nothing but working themselves into life. When they are troubled, they must lick themselves whole. When they are wounded, they run to the salve of duties and the streams of performances, and Christ is neglected. So hard it is to be in duty in respect of performance, and out of duty in respect of dependence! This is a thing beyond their reach, to do all righteousness, and yet to rest in none but Christ. Says the Psalmist to the Lord: 'I will make mention of thy righteousness, even of thine only' (Ps. 71.16). And this is our case, too, for Christ is made to us, wisdom, and righteousness (1 Cor. 1.29).

Thus have I answered the first great query, and the objections that arose from it. I would lay down these two positions as firm conclusions:

1. That the law, for the substance of it, remains as a rule of obedience to the people of God, and that to which they are to conform their walk under the Gospel.

2. That there was no end or use for which the law was given, but such as was consistent with grace and serviceable to the advancement of the covenant of grace.

4

CHASTISEMENTS FOR SIN

———

QUERY 2: *Are Christians freed from all punishments and chastisements for sin?*

If we examine the Scriptures, they seem to hold out this teaching to us, that God's people, those whose sins are pardoned, may yet bear chastisements for sin. That they have at sundry times been under the rod, the corrections and chastisements of God, is plain. Abraham, Moses, David, and indeed all were; and the apostle tells us: 'If ye be without chastisement, whereof all are partakers, then are ye bastards, and not sons' (Heb. 12.8). God scourges every son He receives. That these corrections have been inflicted on them for sin, the Scripture seems to teach in Lam. 3.39–40: 'Wherefore doth a living man complain, a man for the punishment of his sins? Let us search and try our ways, and turn again to the Lord.' Also in Micah 1.5: 'For the transgression of Jacob is all this, and for the sins of the house of Israel.' Also in Micah 7.9: 'I will bear the indignation of the Lord, because I have sinned against him.' Nay, it is laid down as a condition which must of necessity precede God's removal of calamities from them, that they were to humble themselves for sin, and turn from sin before God will deliver them. Thus the Lord speaks to Solomon (2 Chron. 7.14), and thus also do we read in Lev. 26.41: 'If their uncircumcised hearts be humbled, and they then accept of the punishment of their iniquity, then will I remember my covenant.' What does this mean? This: that if they would justify God in His proceeding against them, if they would lie down in the dust and own their punishment, and say that their sins deserved it; if they would acknowledge God's justice in afflicting them; then would God remember His covenant and help them. All this was done by the princes of Israel when they were punished by the hand of Shishak of Egypt (2 Chron. 12.6). It is said, 'They humbled themselves, and said, The Lord is righteous', that is, He justly afflicts us for the sin that we have committed. This proves that they were punished for their sins; for they were to humble themselves for sin under affliction, if they were to justify God in His dealings with them; surely, then, God afflicted them for sin.

But against this it may be said that this was spoken of the whole congregation, and not of those alone who were godly. I grant this, yet the godly themselves were to perform the same duties as the rest; they were granted no exemption; they too were to humble themselves for sin, as we find Daniel and Ezra doing. And if sin was not the cause, and if the calamities were not inflicted on them for sin, then they would have been acting an untruth. To humble themselves for sin as the cause of the going out of God's hand against them, and to accept of the punishment of their iniquity, even while they declared that God was righteous in it, would indeed have been acting an untruth if God was not actually chastening them for sin, and such acting we cannot allow.

Yet, admitting that this was spoken of the entire congregation, we have other Scriptures as evidence that God has punished His own people for sin, including His choicest ones. Moses and Aaron were shut out of Canaan; God would not allow them to enter the land of promise. This was a great affliction; and in Numbers 20.12 it is made clear that the cause of their exclusion was sin, because they had not sanctified God at the waters of Meribah. 'Because ye believed me not, to sanctify me in the eyes of the children of Israel, therefore ye shall not bring this congregation into the land which I have given them.'

David, the man after God's own heart, as God Himself says, is another instance of God's chastisement of a godly man. His child dies, the sword does not depart from his house, his own son rises up in rebellion against him. These were great calamities. The Scripture declares that the cause of them was his sin, his act of murder and his adultery: 'Now therefore the sword shall never depart from thine house; because thou hast despised me, and hast taken the wife of Uriah the Hittite to be thy wife' (2 Sam. 12.10).

DOES CHASTISEMENT PERTAIN TO THE OLD TESTAMENT ONLY?

But against this it may and will be replied that these were examples under the Old Testament, and therefore do not prove our contention, for the godly now live under a different covenant. To this I answer as follows: I have already explained that some divines distinguish between three kinds of covenant –a covenant of nature, a covenant of grace, and a subservient covenant. This last was that which was made with the Israelites at Sinai and was contained in the moral, ceremonial, and judicial laws. It was a covenant which, though it stood upon opposite terms to the covenant of grace, served the purposes of the covenant of grace subserviently. It was a covenant which God made with Israel when they were to enter into Canaan, and it had chief respect to the good or evil which would come upon them in that land. In it God promised blessings upon obedience, and threatened calamities and judgments on them if they disobeyed. All this is set out clearly in the twenty-eighth and twenty-ninth chapters of Deuteronomy. Yet, as I have explained, it was subservient to the covenant of grace, for when they saw that they were neither able to obtain life and outward mercies, nor to ward off death and temporal evils, by their obedience to it, they were to look for the promise of grace and to long for the coming of the Messiah, and to expect all these upon better grounds. Into this covenant they all entered, and bound it with a solemn oath to God, and a curse, as is shown in Deut. 29.12 and 19. God for His part engaged Himself to bless them in the land of Canaan whither they went, if they obeyed His commands; He also threatened to punish them there if they failed to obey Him. To all this they subscribed, and bound it with an oath and a curse. Therefore some interpret the words, 'Do this and live', as if they merely had respect to their well-being in the land of Canaan, and during this life.

I have read a story of the Sadducees who denied the resurrection, and consequently, I suppose, the immortality of the soul. They were men skilful in the law and observant of it, though they held this great error. A certain man, observing their keeping of the commandments, asked them why they kept them, seeing they denied the resurrection and a future life. They answered: In order that it might go well with them in this life, that they might inherit temporal blessings by their obedience to them. I will not say that they served the end of the law in this, for certainly God gave the law for higher ends. But this I may say, that it is possible they served the end of it better than the man who asked the question. It may be that the questioner was keeping the law to be justified by it. We read of such a spirit in Rom. 10.3–4 where the apostle speaks of some who thought they would be justified by obedience to the law, and that was further from the mind of God in giving it than was the motive of those who kept the law that it might go well with them in this life. For the former there is not a tittle of support in the Book of God, but for the latter there seems much. We read of something to this purpose in the fifth commandment: 'Honour thy father and thy mother, that thy days may be long in the land which thou goest to possess.' There is something of it, too, in the second commandment, and a great deal more in Deut. 26.16–19, and throughout the whole of its twenty-eighth chapter; though under these temporal blessings spiritual things were shadowed and apprehended by those who were spiritual.

It is true, the things that were commanded or forbidden were morally good or evil, and therefore of perpetual obligation. Yet the terms on which they seem to be commanded or forbidden, and on which the people obeyed (prosperity or calamity, good or evil, in the land of Canaan), are clean gone. Yet, while the terms lasted, the people were said to break God's covenant by their disobedience. This cannot mean the covenant of grace, for that cannot be broken; it is an everlasting covenant, like that of the waters of Noah (Isa. 54.9). The covenant of grace does not depend upon our walk and our obedience; it is not made upon our good behaviour. Obedience might be the end, but it was not the ground or motive God had in making it. Nor could it be a covenant of works with reference to life and salvation, for that, once broken, is not capable of renewal and renovation. But the covenant under which the Israelites were put was a subservient covenant.

I only suggest this and am not peremptory in respect of it. But I do not see that it will involve us in any difficulties. But (and this is the greatest concession that can be allowed to objectors), admitting that the Israelites were under a different covenant, and that it was of the character we have just explained, yet they were under a covenant of grace also, as well as we. That surely will be granted; for the apostle speaks plainly of it in Acts 15.11 : 'We believe that through the grace of the Lord Jesus Christ we shall be saved, even as they.'

Without doubt, there were some who were God's choice people, who were not only under, but in, this covenant of grace, and yet they were chastised and afflicted for sin – Moses, David and Hezekiah are examples. This objection cannot therefore overthrow our proposition, namely, that God afflicts His own people for sin.

I have already noticed the cavil that the persons I have instanced as having been chastened for sin are taken from the

Old Testament, and that therefore they do not apply to the case as it stands now; but such an attitude actually is full of danger, and would lead to more difficulties than at first appear. The harmony of Scripture must be preserved, for it is one way to discover the truth on doubtful points, and it is the work of the ministers of the Gospel, their great work, to unfold and preserve this harmony, and to show that one part of the Word does not quarrel with and clash against another. The two Testaments are always in sweet harmony and full agreement. God is the same in both; and had we wisdom, we should see the mutualness, the harmonies and the agreements, even in those places that seem to be opposites.

NEW TESTAMENT TEACHING ABOUT CHASTISEMENT

But in this matter I shall meet the cavilling of opponents by showing that the New Testament does nothing but confirm the Old Testament on this matter of chastisement: I think we shall find that both Testaments speak the same language in this matter.

I begin with 1 Cor. 11.30: 'For this cause many are weak and sickly among you, and many sleep.' The apostle here tells them of the fearful sin of profaning the Lord's Table, and of partaking of the ordinance unworthily. Finally he tells them that, though they did not take notice of it, yet this was the great cause of the sickness, weakness, and death which God had inflicted on them, and which now reigned among them. 'For this cause', says he, by which he signifies an unworthy partaking. Can there be a clearer proof of what I am asserting than this? Here we find affliction and punishment set down, and here is the sin set down; and lest all this should not be enough, he tells them plainly that for this sin is this punishment—'For this cause many are sick'.

But it may be objected that this was not spoken of God's

people, but that those of whom it is spoken were unworthy partakers of the sacrament; God's people cannot be unworthy partakers of the sacrament.

In explanation of this matter, observe that there is a two-fold unworthiness, the unworthiness of the person, the unworthiness of present disposition. The unworthiness of the person is seen when a man comes without the wedding garment, unjustified, unsanctified. After this fashion God's people cannot be unworthy for they are not found in this state of unworthiness.

But there is also unworthiness of present disposition, or of the manner of partaking of the Supper, when we do not come with those dispositions and affections which are required in such an ordinance. Habitual preparation there may be, and at the same time the lack of actual preparation, which consists of self-examination, and the excitation of our graces, as the apostle speaks: 'Let a man examine himself and so let him eat of that bread and drink of that cup'; lack of this actual preparation may make a man an unworthy receiver. A similar thing may be seen in the prayer of Hezekiah: 'The good Lord pardon every one that prepareth his heart to seek God, the Lord God of his fathers, though he be not prepared according to the preparation of the sanctuary' (2 Chron. 30.18–19). They had habitual preparation (their hearts were prepared to seek God), but they lacked actual preparation according to the requirements of the sanctuary. Thus may God's people have habitual preparation but yet may lack sacramental preparation.

That the Corinthians were God's people may be seen from 1 Cor. 11.32: 'We are chastened of the Lord, that we should not be condemned with the world.' It was not a punishment, but a chastisement, a term peculiar to saints, and the purpose of it was that they might not be condemned with the unbelievers. This place then is clear enough on the matter. We now look further.

Let us turn to Rom. 8.10: 'If Christ be in you, the body is dead because of sin'. Here the apostle shows that death is the result of sin, and though a man be in Christ, yet he must die because of sin; sin brings death. A saying in Heb. 12.6–8 speaks to the same effect: 'He scourgeth every son whom he receiveth: what son is he whom the father chasteneth not?' And why does he chastise his son? Because he is a son? No, that cannot be the reason. It is because he is a sinner. Correction, though not invariably, here surely implies an offence. So, too, in 1 Pet. 4.17: 'Judgment must begin at the house of God.' With this, compare Rev. 2.12–16, where it is said to the angel of the Church at Pergamos (of whom God gives this testimony, that he had kept the Name of Christ, and had not denied the faith of Christ) that there were some sins among them, and that the Lord bade them repent of them, lest He should come and fight against them. This shows that their sins would bring calamity if they repented not.

And again, in 1 Cor. 10.5–12: 'With many of them God was not well pleased: . . . neither be ye idolaters, as were some of them . . . all these things happened unto them for ensamples, and they are written for our admonition, upon whom the ends of the world are come.' And how are they admonitions to us, if we are not to share with them in the same strokes if we go on with them in the same sins?

VARIOUS CAVILS ANSWERED

Thus have I called your attention to some parts of Scripture which seem to hold out this truth firmly to us, that God's people may be chastised for sin, and that God does chastise His people for sin. Now we shall ask the objectors to show us their strength, so that we may see whether they can stand against the strength and clearness of this truth. We will look first at some of their cavils, which are their forlorn hope, and then we shall look at the main body of their arguments, and

[117]

shall keep strength in reserve to bring to bear afterwards, thus to make the victory of truth more complete and perfect. What then are some of their cavils?

God, they say, does not afflict His people for sin, but chastises them from sin, and they add: the father does not give his child medicine to make him sick, but to take away bad humours, to prevent or remove diseases.

This I regard as a mere cavil. Afflictions have respect both to time past and time to come. God both afflicts His people *for* sin, and chastises them (to use the cavillers' phrase) *from* sin. The father not only corrects his child to make him beware of falling into the fault in the future, but also for the fault already committed. He does it to bring him to repentance and sorrow for his fault, and to work out of him the disposition to it. Or (to use their own similitude), he gives him medicine, not to increase his bad humours, but to remove them. We grant it, and we say, God chastises for sin; not to increase sin, but to remove sin. But we add this, that the reason a father gives his son medicine is bad humours, for if there were no bad humours there would be no need of medicine. Likewise, sin is the cause of the affliction; if there were no sin, there might be no affliction. And if a father may give medicine for the purging out of bad humours before they actually break out, and much more for the correction of them and the cure of them when they do break out, so it is spiritually. If God may afflict men for the purging out of a sinful disposition, much more may He correct them for the actual breaking out of sin in consequence of this disposition. The mistake of the objectors lies here, that they look upon afflictions merely as medicine, and this does not truly answer the case. Afflictions are both medicines and rods. They are called rods (as in Micah 6.9; Job 9.34; Lam. 3.1) because they correct us for sin committed, and medicines to prevent sin in the future. But if a man looks upon them as medicine only, let him remember that medicine has two purposes: first, to purge out our present distemper, which teaches us that afflictions are for sin; second, to promote our future health, which teaches us that afflictions are from sin.

A second cavil is this, that we confound things, and regard that as a cause which is but an occasion for chastisement. God, they say, may take occasion from sin to chastise His people, when yet their sin is not the cause of the chastisement. For instance, consider David's sin in numbering the people of Israel. When he did this, God brought a pestilence upon Israel. David's sin, say the cavillers, was not the cause of the pestilence; Israel's sin was the cause; David's sin was but the occasion; for it is said in 2 Sam. 24.1: 'The anger of the Lord was kindled against Israel, and he moved David against them, to say, Go, number Israel and Judah.' God had displeasure against Israel, and David's sin was not the cause of procuring, but the occasion which God took to inflict this judgment on them. The same may be said of Hezekiah's sin in glorying in the riches of his treasure and the abundance of his store, as appears in Isa. 39.2. He showed all his riches to the ambassadors from Babylon, upon which act of pride and vainglory God sent the prophet to tell him that, as he had thereby tempted God, so also had he tempted an enemy and showed him where he might have a booty if he would only come and fetch it. And that indeed would be the issue of the matter, for all this treasure and show of strength which he had revealed would be carried into Babylon. Now this particular sin of Hezekiah, for which God seems to threaten this calamity, was not the actual cause of it, but at the worst it was but an occasion for it. Therefore it is a great mistake in these and other places to make out those things to be causes which are but occasions. Such is the cavil which we are invited to answer.

Before I answer, let me say that I wish the cavillers were no more guilty of confounding things than we are. Certainly the want of clear conceptions of things has been the ground of those mistakes and erroneous opinions which they have put forth. But we will not recriminate, but proceed to the answer.

We grant as much as this, that this or that particular sin may sometimes be said rather to be the occasion than the cause of affliction. But to this we add that sin is not only an occasion, but it is oftentimes a cause, not only of chastisement in general, but of this or that particular act of chastisement. As is seen in 1 Cor. 11.30: 'For this cause many are weak and sickly, and many are fallen asleep.' See also Ps. 39.11. As for the cases cited by the cavillers, I conceive that they will afford them little success. As for the case of Hezekiah, I am so far from thinking that his particular sin was the cause, that I will not even admit it to be the occasion of the calamities threatened. I grant it to be the occasion of the prediction, but not of the punishment. By reason of his sin, God takes occasion to foretell the calamity which He had decreed, but this was no occasion either of the decree itself or of the evil decreed. As for the other case, that of David, it was not merely an occasion taken, but there was an occasion given by David's sin. It was not only an occasion, but a cause, too. If Israel's sin was the deserving cause, David's sin was the immediate and apparent cause. If Israel's sin procured the affliction, David's sin gave the finishing and concluding stroke. Not only his sin in numbering the people, but the omission of the duty which God required, which was: 'When thou takest the sum of the children of Israel after their number, then shall they give every man a ransom for his soul unto the Lord, when thou numberest them; that there be no plague among them, when thou numberest them' (Exod. 30.12–15). This being omitted, God brought a plague on them.

This is all I shall say for answer to these cavils which are made. I will come next to their main body of arguments.

Their first argument, whereby they would prove that God does not punish for sin, is this: If God takes away the cause, then He takes away the effect also. Sin is the cause of all punishment, punishment is the effect of sin. If God takes away the cause, namely, sin, then too He takes away the effect, which is the punishment of sin. If the body is removed, the shadow goes too. Sin is the body and punishment the shadow; take away the sin and the punishment must needs be taken away. This seems to be implied in that phrase which is used in Scripture for the pardon of sin: 'I will remember your sins no more', that is, never to condemn you for them, nor to charge them against you, nor yet to punish you for them. Where God pardons sin, there He forgives the punishment. This seems to be granted in the thing itself, the pardon of sin. What is the pardon of sin but a removing of guilt? What is guilt but an obligation and binding us over to punishment, spiritual, temporal, eternal? Therefore, if God takes away the guilt of sin, then does He take away the punishment also.

In answer to this argument, it is necessary to distinguish between various kinds of punishments – temporal, spiritual, and eternal. As for eternal punishment, all are agreed that it can never lay hold on those whom Christ has set free, that is to say, those whose sins are pardoned. In respect of spiritual punishments, as they have relation to, or are subordinate to, eternal punishment, so we are freed from them also. Not only so, but we are likewise freed from all temporal punishments as far as they are part of the curse for sin, and as far as they are satisfactions for sin, either satisfaction by way of purchase or satisfaction by way of punishment; for God's justice, both vindictive and rewarding, commanding and condemning, is satisfied. Further, believers are freed from temporal punishments as they are the fruits of sin, or as merely penal, for to this extent are they parts of the curse, and so are inflicted on wicked men, but not upon the godly, all of whose troubles are fruitful, not penal, troubles. As far as temporal punishments are the effects of vindictive justice, and not of fatherly mercy, believers are freed from them. God has thoughts of love in all He does to His people. The ground, the manner, the end of all His dealings with them is love, that He may do them good and make them partakers of His holiness (Heb. 12.10) and hereafter make them partakers of His glory.

But there is another argument which I must answer. It is this: If Christ has borne whatever our sins deserved, and by doing so has satisfied God's justice to the full, then God cannot, in justice, punish us for sin, for that would be to require the full payment from Christ and yet demand part of it from us. Therefore, there can be no temporal punishments for sin.

I grant that God's justice is fully satisfied in Christ. He can require no more that what Christ has already done and suffered. Abundant satisfaction has been made. Therefore, far be it from any to say that God chastises His children for their sins as a means of satisfying His justice. Christ having done that has left nothing for us to bear by way of satisfaction. The Papists indeed say that our sufferings are satisfactions, and therefore they punish themselves and submit to penances. But no Protestant divines say so. We say that God does not chastise us as a means of satisfaction for sin, but for rebuke and caution, to bring us to mourn for sin committed, and to beware of the like.

It must always be remembered that, although Christ has borne the punishment of sin, and although God has forgiven the saints for their sins, yet God may God-fatherly correct His people for sin. Christ endured the great shower of wrath, the black and dismal hours of displeasure for sin. That which falls upon us is a sunshine shower, warmth with wet, wet with the warmth of His love to make us fruitful and humble. Christ drank the dregs of that bitter cup, so much of it as would damn us, and left only so much for us to drink as would humble us for our sin. That which the believer suffers for sin is not penal, arising from vindictive justice, but medicinal, arising from a fatherly love. It is his medicine, not his punishment; his chastisement, not his sentence; his correction, not his condemnation. In brief, then, God, for various reasons may chastise the saints for those sins for which Christ has rendered satisfaction, and which He Himself has forgiven. Augustine names three such reasons – the demonstration of man's misery, the amendment of his life, and the exercise of his patience. I shall give five reasons:

FIVE REASONS WHY GOD CHASTENS HIS PEOPLE

(1) God may do it for the terror of wicked men, that they may read their destiny in the saints' miseries. If it be thus done with the green tree, what shall become of the dry tree? If it thus befall the sheep of Christ, what shall become of the wolves and the goats? If God deals thus with His friends, what shall become of His enemies? If judgment begins at the house of God, where shall the wicked appear?

(2) God may do it for the manifestation of His justice, that He may show to the world that He is just. If He should punish others for sin, but spare His own, wicked men would say that He was partial, that He respected persons. Therefore, to declare that He is just and impartial, He will chastise His own.

(3) God may do it to remove scandal. The sins of the saints bring scandal upon religion; their sins are the sins of public persons; every one stands for many. God was more dishonoured by David's uncleanness than by all the filth of Sodom. The ways of God were blasphemed thereby, as the prophet tells him; and upon that ground, because he had given the occasion, God would chastise him (1 Sam. 12).

(4) Again, He may do it for caution to others. Others' woes

should be our warnings; others' sufferings our sermons, and standing sermons to us to beware of the like. God chastises lest sin should spread to others. The apostle shows this at length in 1 Cor. 10.5–12. Lot's wife was turned into a pillar of salt to season us.

(5) God also chastens His people for their own good here, and for the furtherance of their salvation hereafter. As for the former, it is to humble them the more for their sin. When sin comes clad and arrayed with a cross or sad affliction, then it works the more deeply for humiliation. Afflictions draw men's thoughts inward. It is with the godly as it is with the wicked; sometimes they have a careless ear that can hear indictments against sin, and yet not lay sin to heart. Therefore, God opens their ear by discipline. In their month you shall find them (Jer. 2.24). God's house of correction is His school of instruction. When an affliction comes upon us, then we are ready to listen to the indictments of sin, the checks of conscience, and the reproofs of God, and become ready to abase ourselves and humble ourselves under them. Such is one end in divine chastisements. Another end is to draw the heart further from sin. Another is to prevent the like. Our sufferings will be our warnings. Men who have felt the sting of the serpent, in affliction for sin, will beware of the spawn of the serpent in the pollution of sin. We read that, before the Babylonian captivity, the children of Israel were ever and anon falling into idolatry, and the whole creation was scarcely large enough for them to make idols of. They could scarcely find enough creatures to make idols of. But after God once carried them captive into Babylon, and scourged them soundly for their idolatry, amid all their sins afterwards they never returned to idolatry. Even to this day they abhor pictures.

Many other reasons for the chastisements of believers might be laid down, but the chief is that God chastises them to make them partakers of His holiness here and of His glory hereafter; and, indeed, to sweeten heaven and glory to them. The philosopher Zeno sought torment to assist him to get the most out of pleasure and said that pleasures were nothing worth if they were not thus seasoned: 'from the disagreeable to the esteemed, from thorns to roses, from commotions to peace, from storms to the harbour, from the cross to the crown'. The apostle's words are to the same effect: 'Our light affliction which is but for a moment worketh for us a far more exceeding and eternal weight of glory.'

CONCLUDING CONSIDERATIONS

I shall proceed no further with these unhappy differences between us, but before I conclude this answer will add a few thoughts worthy of consideration.

1. Sin does naturally bring evil upon us. As there is peace and good in the ways of holiness, so there is evil and trouble in the ways of sin. They are never separated. Trouble is the natural and proper fruit of sin, the fruit which it naturally bears. Evil lies in the very bowels of sin. Sin is a universal evil, a big-bellied evil. All evils are born of sin. If you could rip up sin you would find all evil within it. All the evil in punishment lies in the evil which attends upon sin. All the Commandments were given for good, and our good lies in obedience to them. He that breaks the bounds that God sets, necessarily runs into evil and trouble. Sin is born from our hearts, and trouble is born from sin. Trouble is as truly a child of sin as sin is the natural issue of our souls. Not only by consequence and by God's ordination, but naturally, sin brings forth evil and trouble.

2. The evil that sin brings, and the trouble that comes by sin, is either by chance or by providence and Divine dispensation. But it cannot be by chance. Job tells us so, and surely he tells the truth: 'Afflictions do not arise out of the dust' (Job 5.6), and Christ says that: 'There cannot a hair fall from your head', without a providence (Matt. 10.29–30). And if not a hair,

if not the smallest thing without a providence, then much less the greatest. Augustine says that God arranges the various parts of the body of a flea or a gnat. So then, the evil that comes by sin is not by chance, but by providence and Divine dispensation.

3. If evil arises from providence, then either it is from God's active or from His passive providence, or, if you prefer it this way, from either His permissive providence or by His active ordaining providence. The former – permissive providence – does not so well suit with God, who is all act, nor with the words of the prophet: 'Shall there be evil in a city, and the Lord hath not done it?' (Amos 3.6). Understand that this is meant only of the evil of punishment, not of the evil of sin, in which God has no hand. There are many things which God permits in the world, which He does not do; these are the evils of sin. But the evils of punishment, these He permits and does too. Isaiah gives the same answer as Amos in this matter: 'Who gave Jacob for a spoil, and Israel to the robbers? Did not the Lord, he against whom we have sinned?' (Isa. 42.24–25). We see, then, that all these come from Divine dispensation. God brings this evil, and He tells us, too, that it is on account of sin.

4. If God in His providence brings evil upon His people, then either it is out of love, or out of anger, or out of hatred. It cannot be out of hatred, for that were an impossibility; there is nothing that God does to His people that is the fruit or effect of hatred. Indeed, afflictions on the wicked are the fruits of hatred, droppings before the great shower of wrath falls upon them; but it is not so with His own people. Then it is either out of love or out of anger. Certainly it is not out of anger apart from love, for the principle, the ground, the end of all His dealings with His people is love. There is nothing He does to them which is separated from His love; there is love in all. Nay, it is from love that the chastisements proceed: for all his ways are ways of mercy to them that fear him (see

Ps. 25.10). But because afflictions and chastisements are evils, and seem to be the works of one who is angry and displeased, therefore I say that, though they come from love, yet it is from love displeased, from love offended. Paul says: 'God had mercy on Epaphroditus, and not on him only, but on me also' (in restoring him to health) (Phil. 2.27). Why was this? Would it not have been a mercy to Paul if he had died too? Are not God's ways, ways of mercy? And therefore, if he had died, would it not have been a mercy too? What shall we say to this? Shall we say it would have been a mercy in the issue and event, as God would sanctify it to the apostle, and do him good by it, as he himself says, 'All things work together for good to them that love God' (Rom. 8.28)? Indeed this is good, but this is not all; sin itself may be a mercy in the issue. But the Psalmist says: 'All the paths of the Lord are mercy and truth.' Not a step God takes towards His people, not an action that God does, not one dispensation of providence, but it is out of mercy. Therefore, what is the meaning of the saying that God had mercy on Paul in restoring Epaphroditus? Why should he say so, seeing it would also have been a mercy if he had been taken away? Would not God still have showed mercy to Paul even if Epaphroditus had died? Why then does Paul say that God had mercy on him in the restoring of Epaphroditus?

I agree that indeed it would still have been mercy to Paul if Epaphroditus had died, but a correcting mercy, a mercy in chastisement. The apostle seems by this expression of his to imply a medium, or at least a difference between mercy restoring and mercy depriving. It would still have been mercy, but a correcting mercy, if God had taken Epaphroditus away. And so it is in general; though afflictions and chastisements are sent in love, yet because in themselves they are evil, therefore, I say, they proceed often (not always) from love displeased, from love offended. We say indeed that God is angry; not that we are to conceive there is anger in God, for He is without

[127]

'passions' even as He is without 'parts'; but we say He is angry because He deals with us as men are accustomed to deal with their fellows in such cases; they withdraw from them, they chide them, they rebuke them, they correct them. Likewise does God, in a paternal displeasure, act towards those He dearly loves. I must draw to a close in this matter, but I must first mention a few further particulars so as to give full satisfaction to the exercised.

(1) First, God does not for ever chastise His people for sin. I say this, that not all the chastisements which God inflicts upon His people are for sin. Some are inflicted for the prevention of sin, as in the case of Paul's temptation; some for the trial of graces, as in the case of Job. Divines distinguish various kinds of afflictions. Some are chastisements for sin, some accompany witnessing to the truth; some are trials of faith and give exercise to our graces. So that, though it be granted that God chastises for sin, yet not all the afflictions which God brings upon us to exercise us are for sin. It may be truly said that sin is the general cause of all calamities, but it cannot always be said that this or that particular affliction is procured by a particular sin. We see this in the case of the trials which came upon Job and Paul.

(2) God sometimes takes occasion by the sins of His people to afflict and chastise them. Thus far most Christians are in full agreement. Many will grant sin to be the occasion, who will not grant that sin is the cause why God afflicts His people; and indeed, this or that particular sin often seems to be an occasion rather than a cause of the chastisement. Sin may be the cause, and yet this or that particular sin may be but the occasion, as I have showed before.

(3) Not only does God take occasion by sin, but often He chastises and afflicts His people for sin. For sin, I say, and not only for the preventing and the curing of sin, but for the punishment and correction of it, as I have already showed at some length. God makes us to see sin in the effects when we

will not see it in the cause; to see sin in the fruit of it when we refuse to see it in the root. God reveals sin to us through His works, when we refuse to see it through His Word. That which we will not learn by faith, He will teach us by sense: 'A rod is for the fool's back' (Prov. 10.13).

(4) When God chastens His people for sin, His chastisements are not the fruits of wrath or parts of the curse, for there is no wrath in them; they are not satisfactions for sin; they are not sent in vindictive justice; they are not merely penal, but medicinal; their reason is displeased love, and their purpose is fuller embraces.

This must suffice for the answer to the second query.

5

PERFORMANCE OF DUTY

QUERY 3: *If a believer is under the moral law as a rule of duty, is his liberty in Christ infringed?*

The question might well have been divided into two parts: (1) Whether it consists with Christian freedom to be tied to the performance of duty? (2) Whether the Christian is tied to the performance of duty because God has so commanded? We shall find these opinions held: (1) That it is an infringement of the freedom we have by Christ to be tied to the performance of duty at all; (2) That it is far below the free spirit of the saints to be tied to the performance of duty because God has commanded it. We might therefore have dealt with these questions separately, but for brevity's sake we shall regard them as belonging to one question, yet we shall answer both parts distinctly.

We commence with the first part: Whether it consists with our Christian freedom to be tied to the performance of duty? We answer: It is no infringement to our liberty in Christ to be tied to the performance of duty. It was the great end of our freedom and redemption that we might serve God. Christ redeemed us from sin that we might engage in such service, as says Zacharias in his song: 'That we being delivered out of the hand of our enemies might serve him without fear, in holiness and righteousness before him, all the days of our life' (Luke 1.74–75). Christ has not redeemed us from the matter of service, but from the manner of service. He has redeemed us from a slavish spirit in service and brought us into a son-like spirit; from a spirit of bondage to a spirit of liberty. He has broken the bonds of subjection to other lords, that we might take on us the yoke of service to Him whose yoke is easy and whose burden is light (Matt. 11.30). Hence the apostle, after he has set down the main privileges which we enjoy by the redemption of Christ, such as justification, and freedom from the guilt and power of sin, infers: 'Therefore we are debtors, not to the flesh, to live after the flesh, for if ye live after the flesh ye shall die; but if ye through the Spirit do mortify the deeds of the body, ye shall live' (Rom. 8.12–13). The truth is as plain as if written with a sunbeam. It is as easy to separate the sunbeam from the sun as holiness and obedience from the person whom God has justified. As says the apostle: 'The grace of God that bringeth salvation hath appeared to all men, teaching us that, denying ungodliness and worldly lusts, we should live soberly, righteously, and godly, in this present world' (Tit. 2.11–12). So that about the first part of our inquiry there can be no controversy. It does consist with our freedom to be tied to obedience or the performance of duty; nay, it is part of our redemption, and part of our freedom. Indeed, that is true and real bondage which is not joined with sincere and true obedience.

THREE MISTAKES WITH REGARD TO THE PERFORMANCE OF DUTY

But there is some controversy about the second part of the query: Whether it is any infringement of our Christian liberty to be tied to duty because God commands it? Many, though they would perform duty, are disinclined to be tied to it. They would rather perform it as they follow the inclinations of their own spirits than as the duty is imposed upon them by God. There are three mistakes about this matter. We shall consider first the case of those who think they ought only to obey when the Spirit of God moves them to it.

(i) *The case of such as wait for the Spirit to move them to obedience*

Indeed, when the Spirit of God moves, it is good to go, to spread the sails when the wind blows, to open when He knocks. As it was said to David: when he heard the noise in the tops of the mulberry-trees, then he was to go out, for God was gone out before him (2 Sam. 5.24). So when you find strong movings upon your spirits, it is good to take those hints of the Spirit of God, and to close with the season. Many are like harlots who will murder the child in the womb, to avoid the trouble of child-bearing. Similarly they will murder the births of the Spirit, because they would not be at the trouble of the work required by Him. This is a fearful sin, to cast water upon and quench and cool any motions of the Spirit of God. When God moves, He comes with power for the performance of the duty; then we should go full sail. It is good to take such hints. But good hearts in this case sometimes mistake, and become perplexed, and think that if they do not act upon every motion of their spirits, no matter how unseasonable it is, they have quenched and rejected a motion of the Holy Spirit. I conceive it therefore not amiss to tell such that sometimes Satan sets us to the performance of duty when we think it is the Spirit of God that does so. This may seem strange, but yet it is truth. There are four occasions in which Satan usually sets men to duty:

1. When our spirits are much sunk and down, either oppressed with temptations or troubles, then Satan puts us to the performance of duty. It is possible that God also may set us to duty at such times, but sometimes the prompting comes from Satan. He deals with us as the Babylonians did with the Israelites when they were oppressed with their captivity in Babylon, and when they said to them, 'Come now, sing us one of the songs of Sion.' Thus, when the spirit is oppressed and overwhelmed, when Satan thinks that we are at a great dis-

advantage and when he hopes that we shall torture and distress ourselves the more, then it may be he urges us to pray, and not to believe, as those did who dealt with Christ, blinding his eyes and then saying: 'Prophesy, who smote thee?' (Luke 22.64). And so it is with us: when Satan has blinded our eyes, he bids us now see, now prophesy, now pray. When he has disturbed our spirits, when he has troubled the sea (of our souls) that it casts up nothing but mire and dirt (that is, distrustful and unbelieving thoughts), then he bids us go and pray. Yet even so, this sometimes helps to lay the storm, and to quiet the spirit too, so that Satan loses by it. It proves to his own disadvantage, for unexpected grace comes in which he was not aware of, and which he could not foresee.

2. A second occasion when Satan may set us to the performance of duty is when we are called by God to other employments, either natural or spiritual. As for the latter, we may be called to hear the Word, or to confer with others, or to engage in other such duties, and at such times he bids us go to prayer; that is, he loves to make duties clash one with another. Or the difficulty may arise from his use of our natural employments. It may be the occasion of our eating and drinking, or our sleeping. Sometimes he has carried a poor soul out of his bed or taken him from his meat, and told him he must now go to prayer. Yet this may not have been to Satan's advantage either. But thus he sometimes tempts poor souls; and if they do not go to duty upon his instigation, then he tells them they have resisted a motion of the Spirit of God. If they obey him, it is equally for their trouble; it leads to trouble either way. Perhaps he will charge them with Popery and superstition and voluntary penance, if they rise in the night to go to prayer or similar exercises. Who requires this at your hand? he questions. It is good in all such cases to say with a godly man who was thus moved to prayer when he should have been asleep, Get thee hence, Satan, I will go to duty when God calls, not when thou dost suggest; I have com-

mitted my soul into the arms of Christ, and in His arms I will rest and sleep.

3. But there is a third occasion when Satan may set us to the performance of duty. When we are weak in body and not able to perform it, when we lack the natural spirits to do the work, then will he put us on the doing of it. He knows that if we attempt it, then he will, by reason of our natural weakness, get the advantage over us. When he puts us to lift logs, he knows we are weak. When he moves us to duty, it is only because he knows that we have no strength.

4. Another occasion when he puts us upon duty is when he thinks duty will prove a snare to us. In this case he puts us to it, not as the work of God, but as that which will bring us into difficulty, that which will not bring us comfort but rather torment and vexation, that which will not raise us when we are dejected but cast us down still lower. Yet, even so, he is often mistaken.

Thus Satan sometimes sets the believer to the performance of duty. But so, too, does the Spirit of God. He stirs up the heart to duty, and when He moves indeed, He moves effectually; He sets the believer to the duty and gives him strength to perform it; He carries him through. And it is good to observe God's times, the hints of the Spirit, and to go with them. This is my first answer to the mistake of my opponents.

But again, though we are to go to duty when God's Spirit moves us, yet we are not to neglect duty when we do not perceive such sensible motions of the Spirit. Grace moves us, or should move us, to converse with God every day; and if so, it is the Spirit who moves us to it. It is the Spirit who regenerated us, though the Spirit who regenerates us does not Himself appear; and God's Spirit may move secretly, even where He does not move visibly and sensibly to the soul.

Besides, if a person looks for this direct summons to duty, then he will not perform duty out of obedience to the command. We must perform duty at times out of obedience, though we are without both a heart for it and a heart in it. That duty is esteemed by God which is wrested out of the hands of the flesh, and which is carried through against temptations and gainsayings.

Furthermore, if the believer never goes to duty but when the Spirit sensibly moves him to it, he will often lack that communion with God which he now enjoys. How often does a believer go to prayer with a dead heart, and rise with a lively heart! He begins with a straitened heart and rises with an enlarged heart; he begins dejected and ends comforted! How often, when he could find no such motion of God leading him to duty, has he yet met with God in the midst of the duty, and enjoyed God, in a prayer, in a glorious sweet way! 'Thou meetest him that rejoiceth and worketh righteousness, those that remember thee in thy ways' (Isa. 64.5). God loves to meet those that are in His way. Though the miller is unable to command the wind, yet he will spread his sails, and thus be in the way to use it, if it come. Though the lame man could not get into the waters, nor command the moving of them, yet he would lie for thirty-eight years by the waters' side, and undoubtedly with a deal of longing every time the waters moved—O that some would throw me in! So, though we cannot bring the Spirit to us, yet let us set ourselves in the way for Him to meet with us. Maintain the performance of duty; by it the believer may come to see the face of God, to have converse with Him. Thus also he makes headway against sin, gets supplies of strength from Christ, and gets above the world. Those who speak against the performance of duty might as well speak against the actings of faith and the exercise of grace. For prayer is nothing else but the communication of the soul with God, the actings of faith and the exercise of grace. This must suffice for a reply to the first mistake of some, that they are not to perform duty but when the Spirit of God moves them to it.

(ii) *The case of such as think they are to do nothing else but pray*

But there is another mistake. Some there are who think they are to do nothing else but pray. God has commanded us to pray and they think they are to do nothing else. Therefore, ever and anon they run to their knees, drop as it were a head, say over a Pater Noster (Our Father), and with a Popish spirit too, as if they had thus done so much to obtain life, so much laid out for the purchase of a pardon and for heaven. There are too many such persons.

There are two chief kinds of such persons. There are such as are blind and ignorant. They would fain go to heaven, and they hear that they ought to pray. Therefore they go to prayer every moment, determined not to lose heaven for want of prayers. There are others who are in humiliation and wounded in spirit. Poor souls! They go ever and anon to their knees. In some cases doubtless there is the dawning of faith and a desire to seek Christ; but in other cases those who thus kneel do so as a salve to heal their wounds, or as a bribe for a pardon, or as so much good money laid out for the purchase of glory. Naturally, men run to a covenant of works, but it must be another kind of work to bring us to Christ. A convicted man runs to a covenant of works. It is a converted man who embraces the covenant of grace. Thus much for the second mistake.

(iii) *The case of such as think they are to perform duty because their hearts incline them to it*

There is a third mistake. Some there are who think that they are not to perform duty because God commands it, but because their own hearts incline them to it. To this I answer: Though we must perform duties such as praying and hearing because God has commanded us so to do, yet it is not alone sufficient to perform them because God has commanded them. In explanation of this, it must be understood that there are two kinds of laws, laws positive and laws natural. I mean that some laws are founded upon God's will and that others are founded upon God's nature. Those that are founded upon God's will are good because God commands them. Such were many of the Old Testament laws, such as the ceremonies and the forbidding of certain meats. These were things neither good nor evil in themselves, but only as God commanded or forbade them. Some laws, on the other hand, were founded on God's nature and were intrinsically and inherently good in themselves, and not only good because God commanded them.

As for the first of these, namely, those laws which were founded on God's mere will, it was sufficient that men obeyed them simply because God had commanded them. The apostle called them a heavy yoke which neither they nor their fathers were able to bear (Acts 15.10). In so speaking, Peter indicated that obedience to them was more because God had commanded them, than because of any inherent intrinsic goodness which was in them. His calling of them a heavy yoke was a sign that the Jews obeyed them, not out of love to the things commanded, but out of love to that God who commanded them. They were indeed a heavy yoke, but yet they bore it until God took it off. They were hard laws, but yet they submitted to them till God was pleased to repeal and disannul them. And indeed I may well call it submission, for their obedience was more out of submission than delight. And for those laws it was sufficient that they obeyed them merely because God had commanded them.

But as for the other laws, those founded upon God's nature, and which were in their own nature good and holy, it was not sufficient to obey these solely because God had commanded them. It was also required that in men's hearts there should be an inward principle agreeable to them, an inward loving of them and closing with them. These commands must not be esteemed a heavy yoke or a burden, but a delight; and they are to be obeyed from a spirit of love.

When, I say, we are commanded to love God, to fear God, to honour God, it is not enough to do this because God commands it, but there must be an inward principle bred in us whereby we do all this. He that loves God solely because God commands it does not love God at all. If this command be all, then if God has not commanded, he would not do it. But a Christian is to do this though there is never a command to bind him to do it. He sees so much beauty and loveliness in God, his heart is so much taken with Him, that He must needs love Him.

And as for prayer, it is not enough that a Christian man prays solely because God has commanded prayer, but he is to go to the duty of prayer out of desire for communion with God. He goes to the performance of the duty, but not only as it is a duty commanded. Carnal hearts which have no love to the duty perform it because of the bare command. But the true believer goes to prayer because it is a means of converse and communion with God, and he thinks it happiness when he can enjoy a little such communion with Him in the duty. He seeks to converse with God, not as a servant with his master, but as a child with his father; not as a matter of duty, but as his nature calls him to it; not as a service only, but also as a privilege. He esteems access to God and communion with Him one of the highest privileges of a Christian.

FOUR WAYS IN WHICH THE BELIEVER IS FREE FROM DUTY

I agree that Christians are freed from duty by their freedom in Christ, but only in these ways:

(1) We are free from duty as our task. As a task it was a burden to us. We are not like day-labourers in the ways of God, as if we had to earn every penny we have at God's hands. As far as duty is a task, we are free from it.

(2) We are free from duty merely as our trade. We walk in

duty's ways, but not after this fashion, for those who walk in duty as a trade do not follow it for love of the work, but for love of the gains which come of it. A Christian will perform duty because he loves it, even though he sees no gains coming to him by it. The work itself is reward and wages to him. Consider a man who loves sin, whose nature is held in captivity to sin. He will drink and sin though it is to his utter undoing. Just so will a godly man serve his God. He will carry on in the way of obedience even if it yields him no rewards. There is such a suitableness between a godly man and Christian duty that he will perform it though he gets nothing by it.

(3) The believer is free from slavery of spirit in the performance of duty, and does duty out of a childlikeness of spirit, but others perform duty because of the fear of blows or of the cudgel. Were it not for the fear that God would punish them for their omission, they would not go through with the duties. But the godly man would do the duty even if there were no punishment for the omission of it. He counts it his greatest punishment to be denied communion with God. He would speak with God; this is all he asks.

The case of Absalom will serve to a small degree to illustrate this matter. Absalom had been banished from the court and from Jerusalem. Afterwards, through the mediation of Joab, he was allowed to return to Jerusalem, but he was denied admission to the court and communion with his father. Whereupon he sends Joab to mediate for him. The pardoning of his fault was not esteemed so great a mercy as the banishment from his father's sight was esteemed a misery. Therefore he said, 'Let me see his face, though he kill me.' He thought no punishment for his fault to be so great an evil as to be denied access to his father and communion with him (see 2 Sam. 14). So it is here with the soul. The godly man thinks this the greatest punishment, to be denied access to God and communion with Him. Oh, this he esteems to be the height of misery. Rather would he be killed in communion and access to God than enjoy all other kinds of freedom with the denial of such access. A man of corrupt heart does duty because of punishment through failure to perform it. A child of God esteems it the height of punishment to be denied communion with God. He has reached the height of happiness when such communion is his. 'Blessed is the man whom thou causest to approach unto thee', says the Psalmist (65.4), and herein he conceives his blessedness to consist, that is, in approaches to his God.

(4) The believer is free from duty upon the tenders and terms commanded in the law. He does not perform duty that it may go well with him here; nor does he perform duty that he may gain glory hereafter. He regards communion and nearness to God as happiness enough. His spirit does not say to him: Act thus, pray, obey, and it shall go well with thee in this world, and gain heaven for thee hereafter. No! he esteems it a piece of his heaven, to have communion with God. This is 'coelum extra coelum' (heaven this side of heaven). There is enough in the thing itself – communion with God – to induce him to seek it and make his soul desire it. He engages in the duty as if, in itself, it were a part of his reward; and if he can but find God in it, and have converse and communion with God in it, oh, there is heaven enough and glory enough in his soul. As for other prayers of his, in which his soul finds no special communion with God, he has this much comfort from them, that his soul did in such and such a duty set itself in sincerity to converse with and have communion with God, though, miserable and poor man that he is, he failed to obtain it.

NINE DIFFERENCES BETWEEN LEGAL OBEDIENCE AND EVANGELICAL OBEDIENCE

Give me leave to show the differences between the two spirits, the legal spirit and the evangelical, in nine particulars; these will be worthy of notice:

(1) The principle that moves the one spirit to duty is slavish, the other childlike. In one case the man does things in a legal spirit, either hoping to get rewards by it, or fearing punishments if he omits the duty. The godly man, on the other hand, goes about duty for the sake of obtaining communion with God, and knows it to be his reward and happiness to have that communion, while the lack of it is the greatest punishment he can endure.

(2) The one man does these things as his delight, and the other as his burden. And indeed it must needs be burden to them who find not God in prayer, either something of God going out from them to Him, or something of God coming down from Him to them. To the man who has to do with nothing but duty while he is performing duty, to him duty is tedious; but to those who have to do with God, with Christ, in their duties, to them duty is a delight. Though the man of slavish spirit prays, he has nothing to do with God in prayer, he has no converse with Him; he has to do with nothing but duty in duty; yea, and not with duty alone, for he has to do with the world, with sin in duty, not with duty in duty, much less with God in duty. Therefore it is tedious work to him. But the godly man has to do with God. He labours, he breathes, his heart gapes after Him. He it is whom he has in his eyes, and whom he labours after in prayer, even if he cannot enjoy Him.

(3) The one type of man performs duty from the convictions of conscience, the other from the necessity of his nature. With many, obedience is their precept, not their principle; holiness their law, not their nature. Many men have convictions who are not converted; many are convinced they ought to do this and that, for example, that they ought to pray, but they have not got the heart which desires and lays hold of the things they have convictions of, and know they ought to do. Conviction, without conversion, is a tyrant rather than a king; it constrains, but does not persuade; it forces, but

does not move and incline the soul to obedience. It terrifies but does not reform; it puts a man in fear of sin and makes him fear the omission of duty, but it does not enable him either to hate sin or to love duty. All that it does is out of conviction of conscience, not from the necessary act of a new nature. Conscience tells a man that he ought to do certain things, but gives him no strength to do them. It can show him the right way and tell him what he ought to do, but it does not enable the soul to do it. Like a milestone by the roadside, it shows the traveller the way, but does not give him strength to walk in the way. On the other hand, where there is the principle of the Gospel, where there is grace, it is in the soul as a pilot in a ship who not only points the way but steers the vessel in the way which he appoints.

(4) The one kind of man looks for his satisfaction in the duty by the performance of the duty, the other looks for satisfaction in the duty as he finds Christ thereby; it is not in the duty, but above the duty, that he finds his satisfaction.

(5) The one kind of man contents himself with the shell, the other is not content without the substance. The godly man goes to duty as the means of communion with God, to see God, to enjoy God, and to talk with God; the other goes to duty merely to satisfy the grumblings and quarrels of his conscience.

(6) The one type of man performs duty in order to live by it. Ask such a man (for he prays) how he thinks he will get to heaven, and he will say that he will reach it by prayer. But the believer prays and performs duty, yet he looks beyond them, and looks to live by Christ alone. He lives in the duty, but not by the duty; he lives in obedience, but yet looks higher than the obedience: 'I live, yet not I, but Christ liveth in me.' He looks for as much by Christ, and from Christ, as though he had never prayed a prayer or shed a tear. Even though he has done both these things in abundance, yet for his acceptance he looks up to Christ as if he himself had done nothing at all.

(7) The one type of man does things coldly and formally, the other fervently. Yet I do not question but that at times there may be coldness in a godly man and earnestness in the other. If Baal's priests prayed to their idol so earnestly, much more may a natural conscience God-wards. A natural man may pray earnestly. There is no doubt that Ahab was at one time earnest. A condemned man may cry earnestly for pardon. A natural man may pray earnestly at times when in fear or horror, or under pangs of conscience, but he does not cry believingly. There may be much affection in a prayer when there is but little faith; there may be fleshy affections, natural affections, affections heightened either from convictions or fears or horrors. Yet these are but the cries of nature, of sense, and of reason, the cries of flesh, not of faith. Affections based on true faith are not loud, yet they are strong; they may be still, yet they are deep; though they are not so violent, yet they are more sweet, more lasting.

(8) The formal man does duty with a view to it serving other ends, and especially when he finds himself in extreme difficulties. In certain cases things which in themselves are looked upon as most evil may be performed. A merchant may cast all his goods out of the ship in which he sails; not that he looks on the act as in any way desirable — he may cast away his heart with his goods — but yet in a certain case he may submit to it, to save his life. Some men engage in duty in a similar way; they desire holiness but only under great external pressure. They look upon prayer, upon obedience, upon the mortification of their lusts, and such like, as so many hard tasks and impositions which they must submit to if they would come to glory. But it is not so with the godly man. He closes with these duties as his heaven, as a part of his happiness, a piece of his glory. He does not close with them from a necessity of submission, but out of delight; these things are not his penance but his glory and his desire. The other man parts with sin, not because sin is not desirable, for he weeps after it, but because

it is damning. He parts with sin as Jacob parted with Benjamin, because otherwise he would starve; or as Phaltiel with Michal, because otherwise he will lose his head; or as the merchant with his goods, because otherwise he will lose his life. And so he closes with holiness, not out of love and desire for it, but because he must endure it if he would come to heaven at last. But the godly man, on the other hand, parts with sin as poison, as an accursed thing which he desires to be rid of, and embraces holiness as his happiness. He thirsts to enjoy it and to be swallowed up by it.

(9) The one kind of man does duty as a sick man eats his food, not out of desire for it and delight in it, but because he knows that he will die if he does not eat; yet he has no desire or stomach for it. But the godly man does duty after the manner in which a healthy man feeds, not merely because he needs food, but because he desires it and delights in it. The one man engages in duty as if it were medicine, not food. He is reluctant to perform it; he has no pleasure in it; he is driven to it only because he conceives that his soul's health demands it. But the godly man engages in duty as a healthful man sits down to meat; there is delight, desire, and pleasure in the exercise. The godly are as the new-born babes that desire the sincere milk (1 Pet. 2.1).

The one man cries: 'The good that I would do, I cannot do; the evil that I would not do, I do.' The other man cries: 'The good that I have no desire to do, I do; and the evil that I desire to do, I dare not do.' The latter would sin, but dares not because of wrath; he does duty but has no heart for it, because he lacks the right spirit.

DELIGHT IN DUTY

All delight in duties arises from a suitability of spirit in the doing of them. If there is no grace within the heart to answer to the call of duty from without, if there is no principle in the heart agreeable to the precept of the Word, the heart will never delight in them. This, then, is the reason why a godly man conducts himself well in duty, not merely because it is commanded, but because he has the nature which truly and rightly responds to the command. The law of God which is in the Book is transcribed into his heart; it is his nature, his new nature. So that he acts his own nature renewed as he acts obedience. The eye needs no command to see, nor the ear to hear; it is their nature to see and hear. The faculty of seeing is the command to see. So far as the heart is renewed, it is as natural for it to obey as for the eye to see or the ear to hear; as natural to live in obedience as for the fish to live in water or the bird in air.

Thus it is that we do not obey merely because obedience is commanded – the mere command is for such as have no vital principle in them – but we obey from a principle which God has implanted in us suitable to the commands of God. We grant that the command is the rule, apart from our obedience, but grace is the principle within. The heart and the command answer to one another. As face answers face in the water, or in a glass, so it is with the heart and the command; the command is transcribed in the heart. This is the reason why there is so much delight in the godly man's obedience, for it is natural to obey, so far as the heart is renewed. As it is natural for the eye to see and the ear to hear, so it is natural for the renewed heart to yield obedience to the command; and with this obedience comes delight. 'I delight to do thy will, O my God' (Ps. 40.8). Wherein was his delight? The psalmist shows in the words that follow: 'Thy law is within my heart.' Here we see the ground of true obedience; the law was not only his command, but his very nature. If the law is merely our command we cannot delight to do the will of God. We can perform duties but we cannot delight in them, though we may think them needful as something necessary for glory and for heaven; but when once the law of God becomes our very nature, then we come to delight ourselves in obedience and in the ways of God.

Actions of nature are actions of delight. The eye is never weary of seeing nor the ear of hearing; neither is the heart weary of obeying; that is, as far as the heart is renewed or sanctified. So far as the law of God is its nature, so far does it find delight in obedience. God has promised in His covenant of grace to write His laws on the tables of the heart. Those who know nothing of this have the law in tables of stone, and write after it as after a copy; it is a thing outside of them, and the work is hard. But for the godly, God says He will write His laws on the tables of the heart; He will transplant them into the soul; they become the believer's nature. And then obedience does not seem to be a strange command, a law imposed from without, but obedience becomes a natural thing, arising from a law within the heart, the godly man's very nature. From this source springs that abundance of delight in the law which we see throughout Psalm 119. Delight in obedience to God in His law becomes the nature of the man, and so far as that new nature acts, it acts with delight.

I grant that there may be a kind of irksomeness and tedious- ness in us at times as we seek to do those things which yet are natural and full of delight. Though it is natural for the eye to see, and though seeing is its delight – Solomon says that 'the eye is never weary of seeing' (Eccles. 1.8) – that is to be under- stood of a sound eye. If the eye is sore, it may breed a tedious- ness in the eye even when it does that in which it so much delights. Similarly, though it is natural for the soul to obey, and obedience is that wherein it delights, as the fish delights in water, yet if the principle on which it acts from within becomes disturbed and injured, it may breed a kind of irksome- ness, or weariness, or tediousness in the soul in the doing of that thing which it so much delights to do.

This irksomeness may arise from various causes. The heart of the believer may be damped with carnal affections, or it may be pulled back by the remains of corruption. At times it may drive heavily under some vexatious and long-drawn-out temptation; or strange trials may intervene and occasion some sinking of the spirits. And, alas, the cause may be a relapse into sin. Yet, take the saint at his worst, and we find that he has a stronger bias God-wards than others have even when at their best. In the one case there is a will renewed, though for the present a will obscured or in conflict; in the other case there may be some move towards the giving of obedience, but the will is lacking.

Thus much must serve for answer to the third main query. I have plainly showed that it is no infringement of Christian liberty to be tied to the performance of duties, and to perform and accomplish duties, because God has commanded them. The freeness of the Christian consists in this, that he obeys the commands of God, not only because God has commanded them, but out of principles of love and delight, and because he has within his heart a nature agreeable to the things commanded. He prays because God commands prayer, but not only so. He prays because there is a suitableness between his heart and the work of prayer, between his soul and the duty. He has desires after God, and his soul delights in his approaches to, and his converse with, God. Thus have I dealt with the question at large.

6

PARTIAL BONDAGE

———

QUERY 4: *Can Christ's freemen sin themselves into bondage again?*

We are to consider whether the freemen in Christ, or those made free by Christ, may or may not sin themselves into bondage again. Some affirm the one, and some the other. I shall answer briefly.

TWO KINDS OF BONDAGE

There is a twofold bondage; universal bondage, and partial or gradual bondage. We shall consider first the bondage which is universal, that is, the state of bondage, which is bondage properly so called. It is threefold:

Universal bondage

1. It is a bondage to sin, as is expressed in Titus 3.3: 'We ourselves also were sometimes foolish, disobedient, deceived, serving diverse lusts and pleasures'. So also in Rom. 6.20: 'For when ye were the servants of sin ye were free from righteousness'. And again in John 8.34: 'He that committeth sin is the servant of sin'. And again in 2 Pet. 2.19: 'While they promise them liberty, they themselves are the servants of corruption'.

2. It is a bondage to Satan, who is God's jailer, and holds down poor souls under brazen bars and iron gates, not to be broken. He is the 'spirit that now worketh in the children of disobedience' (Eph. 2.2).

3. It is a bondage to the law, both to the rigour and the curse of the law. The law requires hard and impossible things, yea, and that in such severity that it will not accept of the most eminent endeavours without perfect performance. Nor will it accept obedience in much, if a man fails in a little. Neither will it admit of repentance after failure; one breach of the law cannot be made up again, either by a double diligence or by repentance. Such is the rigour of the law.

Souls under the law are in bondage to the curse of the law. It is an extensive and universal curse, extending to soul, body, estate, silver, gold, and relations, as can be seen in Deuteronomy chapter 29. It is an unavoidable curse. A man is unable to obey in all things and therefore is unavoidably shut up under the malediction and curse; as the apostle reasons in Gal. 3.9–11 : 'As many as are of the works of the law (that is, under the law) are under the curse'. And how does he prove it? 'For it is written, Cursed is every one that continueth not in all things which are written in the book of the law to do them.' Here we see the impartiality of the curse–to 'every one'–and the severity of it. It comes upon all under the law who obey not the law, that is, who obey not in every thing. If a man should obey in all things, but have one omission and failing in his life, it would conclude him under the curse. And a man under the law who continues not to obey in all things is cursed. This, then, is the state of bondage, or bondage properly so called.

Partial bondage

There is also a partial or gradual bondage, a bondage in part or in degrees, which is a bondage improperly so called. This is a bondage in respect of comfort, and also in respect of the manner of obedience. And so I shall answer this query in two conclusions.

(1) The first conclusion is that the freeman of Christ, or those that are made free by Christ, shall never again sin them-

selves into the first kind of bondage, that is, into universal bondage or the state of bondage. Christ's freeman can never again become Satan's bond-slave. He shall never more be a servant to sin, for the promise runs: 'Sin shall not have dominion over you: for ye are not under the law but under grace' (Rom. 6.14). Sin may exercise a tyranny, but never a sovereignty. A believer may be carried captive, as the apostle says in Rom. 7.23 – 'bringing me into captivity' – but he is never a willing captive. He may fall into sin, but he will never more be a servant to sin. His ears will never be bored in token of a willing and voluntary subjection to sin.

Nor can a believer ever again be a slave to Satan. Satan may get the advantage of him, but he can never more become Satan's willing servant. Neither can he ever again come under the law, its rigour and its curse. The law can take no hold of him to condemnation. And why? Because he is not under law but under grace. If he can sin himself from under grace, then indeed he is brought once more under the rigour of the law, and its curse. But this is an impossibility. The believer is free. So much for the first conclusion.

(2) The second conclusion is that, though the freemen of Christ cannot sin themselves into a state of bondage again, that is, into a state of universal bondage, yet they may sin themselves into a gradual or partial bondage. This will appear in two particular cases.

(i) A bondage in respect of comfort

The freemen of Christ may sin themselves into a bondage in respect of comfort. This appears in the case of David as seen in Psalm 51: 'Restore unto me the joy of thy salvation'. Men that will not follow the direction of the Spirit of God shall lack the consolations of the Spirit. If they do works of darkness, they must expect to walk in darkness. Though promises of grace are absolute, yet promises of peace and comfort seem to be conditional. Not that our walking has any meriting or deserving power for the procuring of our peace. But this is the way in which God bestows it and continues peace and comfort to us. In the ways of duty we maintain our communion with God, our approaches to Him, our actings of faith and grace; and in these ways, as comfort and peace are procured, so are they continued. Grace is as the fire, comfort as the flame that comes from it.

But as it is with green wood so it is with us. As green wood needs a continual blast to keep it aflame, else it quickly gathers ash and becomes dead, so we must have the continual exercise of our graces. There will be no flame, no comfort, without the exercise of faith, and of grace, and without an obedient walk before God. Promises of grace, as I have already said, are absolute, but promises of comfort are conditional: 'To him that ordereth his conversation aright, will I show the salvation of God' (Ps. 50.23). 'The work of righteousness shall be peace, and the effect of righteousness shall be quietness and assurance for ever' (Isa. 32.17). 'Thou meetest him that rejoiceth and worketh righteousness, those that remember thee in thy ways' (Isa. 64.5). 'If ye love me, keep my commandments. And I will pray the Father, and he shall give you another Comforter, that he may abide with you for ever' (John 14.15–16). 'He that hath my commandments, and keepeth them, he it is that loveth me: and he that loveth me shall be loved of my Father, and I will love him, and will manifest myself unto him' (John 14.21). Here, it is seen, all seems to lie upon condition. So it is in Gal. 6.16: 'As many as walk according to this rule, peace be upon them, and mercy, and upon the Israel of God.' So that if men walk not in the ways of obedience, they may lack comfort, they may lack peace.

The freemen of Christ may sin themselves into a bondage by sin, though not into the bondage of sin. They may sin themselves into a bondage of fear, yea, and a bondage of trouble. Their sin may cost them brokenness of bones, though they shall not sin themselves into a state of bondage again. Though a believer cannot sin away grace, yet he may sin away the evidence, the sense, the comfort of it. Though he cannot sin away his pardon, yet he may sin away the sense of it and the comfort of it. Though he has it, he has no comfort from it. It is as though there was no pardon as far as he is concerned; otherwise we are bound to say a man may have fulness of peace, of assurance, and of comfort, even when he is involved in the highest acts of sin. And some have even said this.

A Christian man may not only sin away the sense and comfort of pardon, but the evidence and knowledge of it, as that place in 2 Peter seems to imply: 'He hath forgotten that he was purged from his old sins' (1.9). New sins bring new fears, new guilts and troubles. All the former foundations and resting places of the soul seem to be shaken; new doubts arise within the man as to whether or not he is justified and pardoned; and these new doubts bring new troubles and fears on the soul.

But some raise objection to this doctrine. They say that this is the Christian man's weakness, for the freemen of Christ are let loose (from the law) to enjoy the free Spirit of Christ. Dr. Crisp[1] speaks thus in his *Christ Alone Exalted*. He says that Christians have free discourse and free society with the Spirit of God, and may hear all the gracious language of God's thoughts, yea, and with application and comfort, and that (as some even say) as they come hot out of sin.

I answer: This is our weakness indeed, but a penal weakness, a weakness which is a chastisement of former wickedness. There are three kinds of desertions which may come to a godly man: conditional, for the prevention of sin, as Paul's seems to be; probational, for trial, and for the exercise of grace, as Job's; penal, for chastisement following the giving way to wickedness, as in the case of David.

In the first two of these cases, it is our weakness indeed,

---

[1] Tobias Crisp (1600–43), an amiable and benevolent Christian of unblemished character was the chief of the Antinomians of the mid-seventeenth century.

but in the third case the weakness is very different. It is brought upon ourselves by indulged sin, a weakness inflicted upon us as chastisement for wickedness committed, as it was in David. His great sin had brought this trouble and weakness upon him.

The Spirit of God is a tender and delicate Spirit. If we grieve Him, He will grieve us. If we will not follow His counsel and commands, we shall lose the comforts and joys that He brings us. 'Your iniquities have separated between you and your God' (Isa. 59.2). Sin does not lead to a total or final separation between God and ourselves; yet it may cause a withdrawment, and breed a distance between God and us. It may cast up such a cloud, that all the faith we have will not be able to see through it, as was the case with David. A passage in Isaiah proves this: 'For the iniquity of his covetousness was I wroth, and smote him. I hid me and was wroth' (57.17). Here we see what troubles the soul draws to itself from the admittance of sin, even ordinary sin. All the former resting places of the soul are no rest to a man. All his former evidences are beclouded and hid so that he cannot discern them.

But it may be said that this is merely his weakness too, as David says in Ps. 77.10: 'This is my infirmity'. I grant that it is our weakness to question former blessings, as for example, if God has given us a well-founded evidence of pardon and of our interest in Christ, we are prone to call everything in question again. But we must remember that there is a weakness that comes to a man on account of his turning aside from God, a weakness that accompanies wickedness. God suffers it to be so, so that His fatherly ends may be accomplished in him. Such a man must be humbled for his sin, and therefore four things come upon him: God does not now look upon him as formerly; conscience does not now speak peaceably to him as formerly; it may be that Satan is let loose upon him to tempt him; it may be that the Spirit of God withdraws because He has been grieved. Then no marvel if the man is in trouble and if his soul lacks comfort.

But some may object and say: It is the man's work, after he has committed sin, to believe; and if to believe, to be comforted. I answer: Comfort is the fruit of faith, and in this respect it is our work to believe. But a man may be able to believe, and yet may not be able to take comfort. A man may rest upon Christ for pardon, and yet upon reflection he may not be able to give evidence that he is thus resting on Him. Also, a man may be able to discern his own acts, and yet his comfort may for a time be suspended. Though it is our work to believe, it is not so properly our work to take comfort. God would have us take comfort in an orderly way, proceeding from believing and mourning, to joy and comfort. God's workings are orderly workings. It is now a man's work, therefore, if he has sinned afresh, to believe afresh, and mourn afresh, and then to receive comfort.

Again, a Christian may be comforted, first of all, in respect of his former justification. His new sin does not cancel his former pardon, though it will interrupt and disturb his present peace and comfort from it. And secondly, he may be comforted in this, that there is mercy enough in God to cover all his sins, grace enough in Christ to cure this fresh sin. And further, in this he is to find comfort, that God does not suffer him to live in sin, but that He has revealed his sin to him, humbled him for it, and brought him back to Christ in whom he may renew his peace and regain his sense of comfort.

But some will object that, if our peace may be interrupted by our ill walk, then peace and comfort do not depend upon Christ, but upon ourselves; that it is not Christ's work but our walk that brings peace to us. I answer: Some distinguish between a peace with God and a peace with ourselves. The peace with God cannot be lost, but peace with ourselves may be forfeited. Others distinguish between a peace of conscience, and peace with conscience. Just as wicked men may have peace with conscience but no peace of conscience, so the godly may have peace of conscience, but not peace with conscience.

Conscience may object and quarrel and dispute, when actually the soul is truly at peace.

Still others distinguish between a real peace and an enjoyed peace. The godly may have a real peace in respect of their state and condition, and yet may not have a sense of peace that they can lay hold of and enjoy. Again, others distinguish between the peace *of* justification, and peace *from* justification. The former, they say, remains inviolate and uninterrupted, even when the soul neither sees nor feels its usual consolations (see 2 Cor. 5.7 and Ps. 49.5), but the latter may be interrupted and disturbed by our manner of walk. And yet others distinguish between a peace of justification and a peace from sanctification. The former, they say, depends no more upon our walk than our justification itself does; but the other depends upon the exactness of our walking. God, they say, does not maintain our peace while we neglect to walk in the ways of peace: 'As many as walk according to this rule, peace be on them' (Gal. 6.16). God always carries on His work of peace and holiness in proportion the one to the other, and the one nourishes and helps the other.

In a word, I conceive that we may distinguish between the foundation and being of a Christian's peace, and the flourishing and well-being of it. The foundation of our Christian peace is not in us but in Christ, not in our holiness but in His righteousness, not in our walking but in His blood and suffering. He is the spring of our peace, and in Him we have peace (John 16.33). He is said to be our peace (Eph. 2.14). But the flourishing and well-being of this peace much depends upon the exercise of our graces and our exact walking with God. It is a peace purchased for us by the obedience of another, but it must be cherished by our own obedience. And indeed, it so far depends upon us, that if we do not walk exactly, even though we cannot sin away our former pardon, yet we may sin away our present peace.

The five-fold peace of a Christian man

There is a five-fold peace that a man may sin away, the least of which is worth a world:

(1) There is a peace which flows from the witness-bearing of our conscience to our integrity and exact walking. Hezekiah enjoyed such a peace when he said: 'Lord, remember now, I beseech thee, how I have walked before thee in truth and with a perfect heart, and have done that which is good in thy sight' (Isa. 38.3). Paul had the same (Rom. 1.9 and 1 Thess. 2.4–6). This peace we may sin away. If we fall into fresh sin, the comforts of our former walking will not bear us up.

(2) There is a peace which flows from the soul's communion and converse with God in duty. There is peace as well as sweetness in every part of holiness, and this peace a man may sin away. All the sweetness and oneness of spirit with the Lord in duty departs from him if he turns afresh to sin, with the result that the soul, formerly comforted, is now interrupted and disturbed in all its approaches to God and its converse with Him.

(3) There is a peace which comes to the believer from the exercise of the grace implanted in him. He cannot give exercise to any grace but some peace and comfort comes of it. When he exercises faith in believing on and closing with Christ, when he repents and mourns for sin, some peace, some comfort, results from these exercises. But a man may sin away this comfort. Fresh sin wounds and disturbs him in the exercise of his graces, and the comforts which flow from such exercises are necessarily interrupted. Nay, if a man can sin away to some degree that measure of grace which he has obtained through his own improvement of grace, much more may he sin away the peace which should flow from this.

(4) There is a peace which flows from the sense and knowledge of God's grace implanted in the soul. When a man is able to trace out the work of grace in his soul, there must

needs be peace and comfort in it. Now this also a man may sin away. He may sin away the sense and knowledge of a work of grace within him. He may so darken and obscure his own evidences of grace by his sin that he is no longer able to read them, nor to discern that there is a work of grace within him. He may now find enough of grace to afflict him, but not so much as to comfort him. His light did not direct him to exact duty before, and now it afflicts him.

(5) There is a peace which flows from the assurance that God is at peace with the soul, a peace which flows from the sense of Divine favour. This peace we may forfeit and lose. Though we cannot sin away our former pardon, yet we may sin away our present peace. Nay, we may sin away the sense and comfort, and even the knowledge, of our former pardon. This may be implied in the words of the apostle: 'He hath forgotten that he was purged from his old sins' (2 Pet. 1.9).

Thus have we proved that a Christian man, a freeman of Christ, may sin himself into bondage in respect of comfort.

(ii) *A bondage in respect of the manner of obedience*

But once more, a Christian may sin himself into bondage in respect of the manner of his obedience. His present state may differ much from his former state. Though he still serves God, yet it is not with that measure of willingness, not with that measure of freedom, cheerfulness, and delight, not with that enlargedness of heart which marked his former service. David, after his sin, desired that he might have the free Spirit of God restored to him. He had not lost the Spirit; the free Spirit was in him; but he lacked that former freedom of spirit. He lacked the operations and workings of God's Spirit. He lacked that comfort in service and that freedom for service which he had enjoyed before. The wheels were now taken off, and he went heavily and sadly in the ways of life. It is natural for the eye to see and for the ear to hear. Acts of nature such as these are actions of delight. But if the eye is sore and the ear at fault, it may breed a weariness and burdensomeness in the doing of the actions of nature. So it is here. If the principle of action within us is wounded, it may produce an irksomeness in the doing of the things in which we formerly delighted. Though sin cannot bring a godly man into the state of a slave, yet it may disable him from serving fully as a son.

Servileness of spirit may be caused by fear, by doubts and unbelief, by grace weakened in its operation by the prevailings of sin, or by the soul's lack of its former gracious convictions and its discouragement in all its approaches to God. Indeed, the man still serves God, but it is more out of obedience than out of delight. He dares not but pray, and yet he finds little heart in prayer. He is now wounded in all his approaches to God. The sweet agreement and co-naturalness which formerly existed between his heart and duty is now gone. The complacency and delight which he previously enjoyed in all his approaches to God and in walking with Him are gone, too. His soul drives heavily in the ways of obedience. He now goes to duty as a sick man to his food. He performs duty rather from the compulsions of his mind than from any natural delight he has in it. Thus it befalls many of the saints in their relapses into sin. They sin themselves into bondage in respect of the manner of their obedience.

This must serve as the answer to the fourth query, whether the freemen of Christ may not sin themselves into bondage. We shall now turn to our fifth query.

7

OBEDIENCE FOR THE SAKE OF REWARD

QUERY 5: *May Christ's freemen perform duties for
the sake of reward?*

THREE OPINIONS RESPECTING THIS
STATED AND EXAMINED

There are three opinions concerning this question:

(1) Some say that we are to do duty, and to walk in the
ways of obedience, that we may merit heaven and glory. We
must fast, pray, and perform good works; and all this with an
eye to glory, as wages for work, and as the reward due to
obedience. And those who believe this perform their works –
their fasting, praying, penances and such like – that therewith
they may purchase heaven and glory.

The Council of Trent pronounces a curse on those who say
that a justified person does not merit eternal life by his obedience. And what would not the proud heart of a man do,
if by doing he might merit heaven? What torments have the
very heathen endured, out of the belief that they would come
to happiness by them? And what would not others do? I have
read of one who said that he would swim through a sea of
brimstone if he might but come to heaven at last. Men would
be at great pains, and would spare no cost, if what they did
might be looked upon as a laying out for heaven, and as the
purchase of glory and the wages for work. The proud heart
of man would fain have that of debt which God has decreed

to be of grace. He desires to obtain that by purchase which God intends to be a free gift.

But such opinions as these have no place in our inquiry. Certainly, though we may do good works, and walk in the ways of obedience and with an eye to the recompense of the reward, yet none of us holds that these things are to be done with reference to our meriting of it. The apostle tells us that it is not of debt but of grace (Rom. 4.4); and again, 'By grace ye are saved' (Eph. 2.5, 8–10). And yet again, 'The gift of God is eternal life' (Rom. 6.23). 'Glory is not the wages of a servant, but the inheritance of a son.' Thus Calvin speaks, while Augustine says, 'God crowns His gifts, not our merits.'

Indeed, what are all our works in comparison with that glory? If all our sufferings are not worthy to be compared to the glory that shall be revealed, what then are our doings? It was a saying of Anselm, 'If a man should serve God a thousand years, he could never by that service deserve half a day, in fact not one moment of time, in that eternal glory.'

We shall therefore cast man's deservings out of our inquiry; it is too gross for Christian ears. The apostle tells us plainly: 'Not by works of righteousness which we have done, but according to his mercy he saved us' (Tit. 3.5). 'Not by works of righteousness', that is, not by our own works, even though we were to say, as some of the more moderate of our adversaries do, 'our own works sprinkled with the blood of Christ'. All are injurious to grace. For by grace are we saved, and grace is in no way grace if not every way grace. But here we leave such adversaries, and turn to other opinions which are to be debated.

(2) Some say peremptorily that we must have no eye, no respect to heaven and glory, in our obedience. We must walk, they say, in all the ways of obedience, with this freedom, carrying no respect to the recompense of the reward at all. They say it is utterly inconsistent with the free spirit of a

Christian, and destructive of his Christian freedom, to do duty with respect to reward.

(3) There is a third opinion that says we may do holy actions and walk in the ways of obedience, and may also, in doing so, cast an eye upon, and have respect to, the recompense of the reward.

These two last opinions need examination. We have rejected the first opinion as quite inconsistent with the nature of grace and the freedom of the Gospel; but these two other opinions are held by some as consistent with grace and Christian freedom. Yet these two seem to be mutually contradictory. One of them says that we are to do holy service and not to cast an eye upon the recompense of the reward. The other says that we may have respect to the recompense of the reward in the performance of holy duties.

The first opinion, that we are not to have respect to the recompense of the reward, is supported by the following arguments:

1. Because it overthrows the nature of our obedience and makes that mercenary and servile which should be son-like and free. If we obey God in reference to heaven and glory, we do not obey freely, we do not serve God for what He is in Himself, but servilely and mercenarily, our obedience being servile in principle and mercenary in its end.

2. Because a respect to the recompense of the reward in obedience overthrows the nature of grace, and makes that to be man's purchase which is in reality the freely bestowed gift of God. The nature of grace must needs be overthrown by this.

3. Because all the blessings we inherit are included in the covenant of grace made on our behalf. Says God: I will give you grace, I will pardon your sins, I will give you glory. Now we do not obey that we may have pardon, nor obey that we may have grace. Why then the other? Why should man say that he obeys that he may have glory, seeing that this is also similarly promised?

4. Because all the blessings we seek are fully purchased by Jesus Christ and provided for in Christ. Therefore they are not our purchase. We do not obey that we may get this or that; but because glory is purchased for us, and we are persuaded thereof, therefore we obey the commands of God.

As for the other opinion, that we may rightly have respect to the recompense of the reward in our obedience, it is managed and defended by the following arguments:

(1) That which God has propounded as an incentive to obedience, we may rightly have regard to as we render obedience: and indeed God has so propounded it. If motives may be found in the Word to quicken us to obedience, then certainly we may keep them before us in our obedience. But God has without doubt presented glory and heaven as a motive to quicken us to obedience, as may be proved from Rom. 8.13: 'If ye live after the flesh, ye shall die: but if ye through the Spirit do mortify the deeds of the body, ye shall live.' And again in 1 Cor. 15.58: 'Therefore be ye steadfast, unmoveable, always abounding in the work of the Lord, forasmuch as ye know that your labour is not in vain in the Lord.' See also 2 Peter 1.5–12, and 3.14: 'Seeing ye look for new heavens and a new earth, be diligent that ye may be found of him in peace, without spot and blameless.' In Gal. 6.8–9 also we read: 'He that soweth to the flesh shall of the flesh reap corruption, but he that soweth to the Spirit shall of the Spirit reap life everlasting. And let us not be weary in well doing; for in due season we shall reap, if we faint not.' Also 2 Tim. 2.12: 'If we suffer with him, we shall also reign with him.' Therefore, God having propounded this as an incentive to obedience, we may eye it and have respect to it in our obedience.

(2) That which the saints and people of God have eyed in their obedience, we may eye also; and it is certain that they had respect unto the recompense of the reward. We read of Moses in Heb. 11.25–26: 'He chose rather to suffer affliction with the people of God than to enjoy the pleasures of sin for

a season; esteeming the reproach of Christ greater riches than the treasures in Egypt: for he had respect unto the recompense of the reward.' But it may be said that Moses was a man under the law, and that he had not so free a spirit in service as have those who now serve under the Gospel. But to this it may be answered that he was certainly a son, though under age, and that he had the free spirit of grace, else he could have had no glory. Paul also commends this act of Moses to show the greatness of his faith and obedience, and in this respect he sets it forth for our imitation. Furthermore, we shall find that those who were under the Gospel and who enjoyed abundance of God's free Spirit, yet had an eye to the same recompense of reward in their obedience. We find Paul, who had as free and sincere principles in him as ever man had, saying of himself in Phil. 3.13-14: 'I forget all things that are behind, and I reach forth unto those things that are before. I press hard to the mark, for the prize of the high calling of God in Christ Jesus.' See also Heb. 12.1-2.

Thus I have set forth the various opinions of others and the arguments by which they support them. Now, by way of reconciliation, and in order to show that which I myself apprehend to be the truth in this controversy, I shall speak of three matters: what is meant by reward; what is meant by the eyeing of the reward; and whether the eyeing of the reward is in any way an infringement of Christian freedom.

WHAT IS MEANT BY REWARDS?

First we shall consider, What is meant by rewards? Rewards may be said to be either temporal, or spiritual, or eternal. Temporal rewards are those mercies which we enjoy in this present life, whether personal or relative, and these in turn may be positive or negative – health, comfort, food, raiment, house, shelter, riches, freedom, deliverance, and so on. Spiritual rewards are the blessings which concern the soul – justification, sanctification, grace, the increase of grace, victory over our lusts, comfort, peace, joy, communion with God. Eternal rewards, which are the main consideration in this controversy, are glory, life, immortality, as the apostle names them in Rom. 2.5–7: 'God will render to every man according to his works; to them who by patient continuance in well doing seek for glory and honour and immortality, eternal life.' In a word, this eternal reward is the enjoyment of God, of Christ, of the Spirit. It is perfect freedom from sin, it is perfect holiness, it is indeed grace glorified. This is the true eternal reward. This must suffice for the first point.

WHAT IS MEANT BY THE EYEING OF REWARDS?

What is meant, in the next place, by the eyeing of the reward? It is the phrase which the apostle uses of Moses who had respect unto the recompense of the reward (Heb. 11.26). We must explain what is intended by this. There is a threefold eye: the eye of knowedge, whereby a man sees and knows the excellency of a thing; the eye of faith, whereby he believes the truth of it, and his interest in it; and the eye of hope, and thereupon of patience and waiting in expectation for the enjoyment of the promise. In all these respects Moses may be said to have eyed the recompense of the reward.

Moses eyed it by knowledge. He knew those things which were laid up for him. He saw Him that was invisible, as the next verse tells us. And he saw that those rewards which God had laid up for His people were much to be preferred to the pleasures of sin. He also had the eye of faith, whereby he was persuaded both of the truth of the promise, that such things were reserved, and of his own part in them, and that he should possess this glory. Also, he had an eye of hope; he was willing to wait, and to expect the enjoyment of all this. He was patient. See Heb. 10.36: 'Ye have need of patience, that, after ye have done the will of God, ye might receive the promise.'

For these reasons, Moses esteemed the reproach of Christ above all the treasures of Egypt, for, says the text, he had an eye to the recompense of the reward. What is that? Shall we say that he had respect to that glory which he should purchase or enjoy by doing this, or for doing this? No! It was because he knew that the glory was reserved for him, because he believed that he should possess it, because he hoped for it and expected it. That is why he despised the riches and pleasures of the world, as not worthy to be compared with it. Agreeable to this truth are the words of Col. 3.23–24: 'Whatsoever ye do, do it heartily, as to the Lord, and not unto men: knowing that of the Lord ye shall receive the reward of the inheritance: for ye serve the Lord Christ.' See also Heb. 10.34: 'Knowing in yourselves that ye have in heaven a better and an enduring substance'. Thus much for the second matter.

IS THE EYEING OF REWARDS AN INFRINGEMENT OF CHRISTIAN LIBERTY?

We now come to the third point for consideration; whether to do duty with an eye to the recompense of the reward is any infringement of Christian freedom. I answer: If a man is prepared to look at the matter as I have just been explaining it, and to consider the knowing and the believing and the hoping for that glory which God has promised the believer, then, I say, it is no infringement of our Christian liberty to do duty with an eye to the recompense of the reward. Rather would I say that herein our Christian liberty consists, that the knowledge, the faith, the persuasion, the hope and expectation of the glory which God has reserved for us, all conspire to quicken us in our obedience and thereby to make us free indeed in our obedience to God.

In brief, then, if a man is prepared to take this eyeing of the recompense of reward in the manner which I have said, then a man may do duty with an eye to the recompense of the reward. And indeed a Christian should act thus. Duty should be performed with the knowledge and faith and persuasion that God will bless us and never depart from us in doing us good. We know, too, that God is our father and that He has pardoned our sins. We know that God will glorify us at last. With such knowledge, we are to obey and give up ourselves to all the ways of obedience, love and service of God, as the apostle says, 'And whatsoever ye do, do it heartily to the Lord, knowing that of the Lord ye shall receive the reward of the inheritance' (Col. 3.23–24). If, on the other hand, a man takes the eyeing of the reward to mean that it is a method of obtaining temporal, spiritual, and eternal mercies, then I must pause and answer by making some distinctions.

With reference to temporal blessings

We shall consider the matter first in respect of temporal blessings. Some affirm that it is right that a Christian man should do duty to God with a view to receiving from God His outward mercies and the enjoyments of this present life. I know that this opinion is upheld by holy and learned men, who, in their own walk nevertheless seem to pay but scant heed to the recompense of reward. They maintain that God has propounded these rewards as motives and incentives to obedience, and that the best of saints have eyed them in their obedience; therefore they may do the same. To take off all suspicion of mercenariness of spirit in so doing, they are apt to distinguish between supreme grounds and ends in service, and subordinate grounds and ends. They say that though the things of this life may be the subordinate ground and end of such service, yet they are not to be the ultimate and supreme ground and ends of service. We may eye them with reference and subordination to God's glory and our good and salvation, but not so as to place them in the forefront, as if they were above the glory of God and our salvation. These are the usual cautionary distinctions put forward by the men who hold to this position.

I respect the persons and judgments of such men, although what I advance may be somewhat different, yet I do not suppose that it will be altogether contrary to that which they have maintained.

I shall at this point re-state the query, which is, whether a man may do duty and obey God in reference to God's bestowing temporal good things on him. I conceive, first, that the man named in the query must be taken for a Christian man, or a man in Christ. If the query is concerned with a carnal man, it must be understood that such a man neither obeys God from right principles nor upon right grounds, nor after a right manner for right ends. We may say of all his obedience that it is but carnal. The man has carnal principles, grounds, and ends in all that he does. It may truly be said of him what God said of the Jews when they fasted and prayed, they did not at all do this as unto God—see Hosea 7.14: 'They assemble themselves for corn and wine, and they rebel against me'. These Jews merely sought belly-blessings; self was the ground, and self was the end of all. They did not serve God because of what He is in Himself, but for their own advantage. They sought not Him but His, as with those who followed the Lord because they did eat of the loaves and were filled. There are many thousands who are moved, not by any inward spring of obedience, but by these outward matters. As with a clock which is worked by outward weights and cannot move when these are taken away, so it is with such men, who stand still and cannot stir. The carnal heart cries, 'Who will show us any good?' They count godliness no gain, if they can make no gain of godliness. If, instead of gain, they meet with loss; if, instead of advantage, they meet with persecution; if, instead of a good name, they meet with reproach for Christ; then they immediately cast off religion and obedience. They take up with religion merely to serve their own ends, and for similar ends they disclaim it. He that will serve God for something will serve the devil for more. If he can increase his wages, he is for any master. Therefore, by 'man' in the query, I conceive is meant a Christian man, or a man in Christ.

By the 'good things' of the query, I conceive is meant outward good things, those things which the world reckons and esteems to be good things, as riches, honour, greatness, applause; at least, a competency and a sufficiency of temporal and outward good things.

By serving God or performing duty to God, as mentioned in the query, I conceive is meant all acts of obedience, not only outward conformity to God's requirements, but inward subjection to the laws and commands of Christ.

By the eyeing of these temporal good things in service, I conceive is not meant the making of these things either the main reasons for service, or the supreme and primary ends and aims of service, for that would be abominable, but the having a respect unto the enjoyment of temporal good as a subordinate reason for serving God, and a means of quickening the Christian man in working. Thus, then, we have examined the nature of the query. I shall now come to the answer, and in this I hope that the three following particulars will be agreed:

(1) That the enjoyment of these good things in this life is not the ground of a Christian man's obedience. They are not that which sets him to do service to God, even though they may quicken him in service. They are not the spring of motion. At the most they are but oil to the wheels to keep them in motion and to inspire motion. I conceive that there are several grounds of Christian obedience:

1. The binding grounds. The Christian obeys because God has commanded, as we have it in Ps. 119.4–5: 'Thou hast commanded us to keep thy precepts diligently. O that my ways were directed to keep thy statutes!'

2. The enabling grounds. The Christian man is enabled to obey because of his implantation into Christ. As without Christ he can do nothing, so in Christ he is created unto good works, and he can do all things through Christ who strengthens him. The Christian man is also enabled to obey because of the implantation of Christ into him, which is called the forming of Christ in the soul, the new man, the law written in the heart, the new creatures, faith and love, whereby he is enabled to obey God's precepts. His faith enables him—by faith Abraham obeyed—and love constrains him.

3. The impelling grounds. These may rather be termed motives to obedience. The man obeys because God is good, and because He is good to him. God's goodness is a motive, and His grace is the Christian man's strength.

(2) It will be agreed too, doubtless, that the enjoyment of temporal good is not the immediate end of a Christian's obedience, for, if so, it renders him servile and mercenary in his obedience, and not son-like and free. Indeed, such ends may be the mark of the carnal man, but not of the godly. The godly have higher ends than these. These ends are too low for the noble and royal spirits of saints.

(3) It will be agreed, too, that temporal good things are not the main ends of a Christian's obedience. He has higher ends than these. He has a more noble spirit, a more free-born soul, than will permit him to make anything he receives from God the main end of his obedience to God.

So far there is general agreement. All the controversy is about the next point. I desire to propound it in all modesty for the consideration of those who are of different judgment in the matter.

We are to consider whether the performance by a Christian man of duty to God may have reference to God's bestowal of outward mercies on him in this life, considered as a subordinate end. Consider the following points:

(1) To be obedient to duty by the prompting of a temporal reward seems to belong to the work of the law as a schoolmaster. In time of law the godly seemed to be moved to the ways of obedience by promises of temporal blessing, and God seemed to propound to them as men under age the promises of temporal good things to tempt them on to obedience: as appears in Deuteronomy, chapter 29. Certainly, the enjoyment of these temporal things was not the only end of their obedience, though some of them may have had the spirit of the Sadducees who said that they kept the law and observed it in order that God might bless them, and that it might go well with them in this life. Yet all were not of this spirit, nor was the enjoyment of temporal good the main reason for their obedience, any more than it is ours. It was but a subordinate end; God never propounded it, nor did godly men eye it as the main end of their obedience. But God deals with them as with those in infancy, as under age. He leads them on, and allures them by such considerations as these, for they had not the measure and abundance of the Spirit which He bestows on His people now under the Gospel.

(2) Duty done for reward, even as a subordinate end, seems to lay down a rule for God to follow. It seems to limit God, and to depart from submission to His wisdom in His disposal of us.

(3) It also seems to propound that which God has not propounded.

(4) Also, the temporal good things for which the man looks may not be granted, and so far as obedience depends on them, it too will fail.

(5) It is hard to have an eye to the reward of temporal good, and yet for our service to be free.

(6) I conceive that it is safer to find arguments to quicken us in our obedience from the mercies of God bestowed upon

us, or made ours in the promise to faith, than to find arguments to obey from the expectation of mercies to be bestowed as the reward of our obedience. It seems better to say that we are not to obey in order that God may bestow blessings upon us, but rather that we obey from the knowledge, the faith, and the persuasion, that God will bless us here and for ever. It is this latter that quickens us to obey God.

The apostle seems to speak after this manner in 2 Cor. 7.1: 'Having therefore these promises, dearly beloved, let us cleanse ourselves from all filthiness of the flesh and spirit, perfecting holiness in the fear of God.' He argues here from mercy to duty, not from duty to mercy. He reasons here from the enjoyment of promises to the performance of obedience: 'Having therefore such promises, let us obey'. Likewise in Col. 3.24: 'Whatsoever ye do, do it heartily as to the Lord and not to men; knowing that of the Lord ye shall receive the reward of the inheritance.' Here the apostle enforces the duty from the persuasion and knowledge of Christians that God will assuredly bestow the blessings on them. So, too, in Heb. 10.34: 'Ye took joyfully the spoiling of your goods, knowing in yourselves that ye have in heaven a better and an enduring substance.' However, I am not to deal at this point with eternal, but with temporal rewards, and I urge these Scriptures no further than to strengthen what I said before, that it is better to say we obey from mercies promised rather than to say that we obtain mercies by our obedience. Certain it is that the less we seek to obtain mercies because of our obedience the more will God have an eye to our obedience; the less regard we have to the temporal rewards in our service, the more will God have respect to that service; the less we make temporal blessings the end of our service, the more value will God see in that service. Indeed the enjoyment of outward things seems to me to be too low a principle of action in a Christian's obedience. The apostle says, 'We look not at the things which are seen, but at the things which are not seen: for the things which are seen are temporal; but the things which are not seen are eternal' (2 Cor. 4.18).

But it may be objected that God has promised all good things to obedience, as the apostle tells us in 1 Tim. 4.8: 'Godliness is profitable unto all things, having promise of the life that now is, and of that which is to come'; and therefore it is right to obey with respect to the enjoyment of these blessings.

Before I answer this objection, I will propound one thing, and query two. That which I propound is this: Whether it were not better to express the matter by saying that God has promised to the obedient all good things, rather than to say that He has promised them to obedience. This I suggest the more especially, if that be a truth, that God's promises under the covenant of grace are not made to the work, but to the worker; not to the action, but to the person performing it. I am sure that our divines have drawn this one great difference between the covenants of work and of grace, that in the covenant of works made with Adam, the promise was made to the work, not to the person; whereas in the covenant of grace, the promise is made to the person, not to the work.

The two things I query are these:

1. Whether that which the apostle calls 'the promise of this life', and that which is expressed in the Objection under the name of 'good things', are expressions which point to the same thing.

2. Whether by 'good things' is meant those things which are good in the eyes of men, or those things which are good in the estimation of God. In other words, whether is meant those things which are good in themselves, or else those things which God in His wisdom knows to be good for us.

If 'good things' is taken at large and indefinitely, the first part of the Objection is granted; that God has promised to the obedient, or to the obedient in their obedience, all good things. It is His promise as given in Ps. 84.11: 'No good thing will he withhold from them that walk uprightly'. Nay, we have His covenant, in Jer. 32.40: 'I will never depart from them to do them good'. But if it is decided that 'good things' only refers to those things which are positively good, those things which the world esteems good, and does not include wants as well as enjoyments, straits as well as fulness, poverty as well as prosperity, as among the 'good things', then I say that God has made no such promise to the Christian, nor can we truly interpret the promise after this fashion. If it were a promise made to obedience and godliness, and if it were to be interpreted in this way, then surely the apostles themselves would have been sharers in it. But Christ tells them plainly 'that they should be hated of all men for his name's sake, and should be brought before princes, cast into prison, and perse-cuted', and that those who did such things to them would think that they did God good service (Matt. 10.18, 22; Luke 12.11; John 16.2). And the apostle tells us: 'The Holy Ghost witnesseth . . . that bonds and afflictions abide me' (Acts 20.23). He adds: 'If in this life only we have hope in Christ, we are of all men most miserable' (1 Cor. 15.19). And these things we too are to expect and reckon on, according to the saying of the apostle: 'All that will live godly in Christ Jesus shall suffer persecution' (2 Tim. 3.12). Also, 'Through many tribu-lations we must enter into the kingdom of God' (Acts 14.22). Christ Himself tells us that if we will follow Him, we must take up our cross daily (Luke 9.23). Therefore it is certain that if by 'the promise of this life', is meant the good things of this life, and if by the good things of this life is meant outward enjoyments, then I say, there is no such promise made here to obedience.

But it may be asserted that the Scripture says, 'If ye be willing and obedient, ye shall eat the good of the land', and therefore temporal blessings are promised in return for obe-dience. I reply: If it be admitted that the Jews (though under the covenant of grace) were at the same time under a different covenant from us, a subservient covenant as I have already showed, in which God promised outward mercies to obedience and threatened afflictions to the disobedient, then my answer is soon made. David might well say that he never saw the righteous forsaken, nor their seed begging bread, for outward mercies were the conditions annexed to their obedience and to God's part in the covenant, and these failed not to them that obeyed. But whatever it was then, it is not so now. Those who are willing and obedient do not now eat the good of the land. Indeed, it may be that they are in the greatest outward trouble and necessity, whereas they who do wickedly prosper.

Where is it that God has made the promise of temporal good now under the Gospel? If so, why is it not universal and infallible in its application? Why do not those who are willing and obedient enjoy it, and not only some, but all of them? For promises are not made to particular persons, but to the whole body of Christ. Indeed, God tells us now that they that will live godly must suffer persecution, and through many tribulations must they enter into the kingdom of God. Yet this remains firm in all conditions, that God will never depart from us or from doing us good. He will never leave us nor forsake us. In blessing He will bless us. All things shall work together for the good of them that love God. This stands firm and unmoveable to all saints. Heaven and earth shall sooner pass away than one tittle of this promise fail.

But another objection may be raised. It may be said that, if blessings are not promised to obedience, and if God does not reward obedience, then by the rule of contraries, punishments are not threatened against sin, neither does God punish for sin. I answer briefly: God may punish sin, and yet not reward obedience. In our obedience, even if it were perfect, we do but what we should do, as Christ hints to us in Luke 17.10: 'When ye shall have done all those things which are commanded you, say, We are unprofitable servants; we have but done that which was our duty to do.' But when we sin we do that which we should not do; and therefore may God punish the one, and yet not reward the other. The punishment of our sin is but the just demerit of our evil; but the reward of our obedience is the gift of His own mercy. The apostle tells us this when he says: 'The wages of sin is death, but the gift of God is eternal life through Jesus Christ our Lord' (Rom. 6.23). Man may provoke God to show His justice, but he cannot tempt God to show mercy. Our sins draw out His justice, but His mercy is the issue of His own heart. We can do that for which God may damn us, but we cannot do that for which He may save us. Thus it will appear that, though the two parts of the argument taken separately may be granted to be true, yet the conclusion that is drawn from the linking of them together lies open to just exception.

But again, it is granted that blessings are promised to obedience, and that punishments are threatened to sin. But shall we judge nothing to have the nature of blessing but the enjoyment of temporal and outward good things? May not losses be blessings as well as enjoyments? And may not enjoyments be punishments, when yet losses are blessings? Certainly they may be so in truth, though not in name. They may be so in God's intention, though not in our apprehension. And to speak truth, nothing is against us but what is an obstacle to our eternal happiness, and nothing is for us but what is advantageous to it.

Once more: It is granted that God rewards obedience and punishes sin. But it is one thing for God to reward obedience, and another thing for man to have an eye to reward in his obeying. It is granted that reward is the outcome of the work, but it is disputed whether it should be the end which the worker has in view, and upon the considerations propounded. And though God rewards obedience and punishes sin, yet, just as we do not avoid sin because of temporal punishment, so we do not perform duty for the sake of reward. I say 'reward', in the sense of temporal enjoyments. I am unwilling for anything to be introduced as a motive for the obedience of a godly man which is either unsuitable, too low, or uncertain, and temporal rewards seems to be such. They are unsuited to the spirit which underlies the godly man's service, and they have the nature of uncertainty, for we have no absolute promise of them. If there be such a promise, why is it not both universal and infallible? This much must serve for answer to the first part of the objection.

We now come to the second part, which is inferred from the first: that if God has promised all good things to obedience, then we may obey with a regard to the enjoyment of them. I answer by way of denial of this consequence, for, even if it be admitted that God has promised all good things (the 'good things' to be interpreted as before) to obedience, yet it does not follow that the godly are to obey God with a regard to the enjoyment of them. Even if we grant that the apostle, where he speaks of 'godliness' (as being profitable for this life) means 'obedience', or godliness in practice, and by 'the things of this life' he means 'all good things', and these were things positively good, yet we must not obey that the promise may be fulfilled to us. Rather, having this promise, we must be quickened to obey. Certainly the apostle's reasoning is the best reasoning; and he reasons thus: 'Having therefore these promises, dearly beloved, let us cleanse ourselves from all filthiness of the flesh and the spirit' (2 Cor. 7.1). He does not bid the godly do this that they may have such promises; but, as they have such promises, let them obey. Let it not be thought that I would hold the believer back from obedience, or take away an incentive to obedience, or speak against that which would quicken him to obey. But this I say, that the promise of temporal good things, such as riches and prosperity, does not belong to the believer under the Gospel; in its place is mercy and blessing. Furthermore, I conceive that it is a far greater advantage to obedience, and a far greater spur and incentive to obedience, to consider the promise as already made, so that we are not to obey that we may have the promise, but, having the promise (and in 2 Cor. 7.1 the apostle speaks of 'the promises'), how much more should we obey it!

To the further objection that, though we are not to obey that we may have the promise, but that we should obey with a view to receiving the good things included in the promise, I would reply thus:

The things of this life are no part, not so much as a pin, of the workmanship of a gracious soul. They are too low to move one wheel of a Christian's frame. At best they are but oil to the wheel, and oil is not the source of motion, but merely a help in motion. The things of this world can neither be the reason nor the object of the obedience of a gracious heart. They neither set us to work, nor do they keep us working. The enjoyment of them may come in to quicken us to work, and in work; but that is all. 'If thine eye be single, thy whole body shall be full of light' (Matt. 6.22). Likewise the contrary is true. If the eye is double, if our aims and ends take the place of God, the whole man is darkness. In brief, the less respect we have to temporal blessings in our obedience, the more free and noble is our obedience. It is as one says of desire: 'He that desires this on account of that, does not desire this, but that.' So it is with him that obeys in the hope and expectation of receiving outward blessings: either he would not obey, or he would not so cheerfully obey, if there were no such good things to be enjoyed.

But some may say that the godly may pray for these outward blessings, and therefore they may perform duty in respect of them. I answer: it does not so follow. The requirements of our duty and the reasons for the performance of our duty are different matters. We grant that outward things may be requested by us in our prayers, but they do not constitute the true ground of our praying. Besides, we must distinguish between that which is the true motive of our Christian life as a whole, and that which may constitute the motive and end of a particular duty. The latter may be prompted by the hope of outward and earthly good. Thus we may lawfully go to prayer for this end, to make known to the Lord our temporal necessities. Nay, our present wants may be the main and particular ground for performing a particular duty at a certain time. But no hope of worldly and outward blessing can be the hinge upon which the whole frame of our Christian life moves. Outward blessings may be the ground of particular acts, but not the main-spring of the whole. They may be the particular end of a particular duty, but not the general end of the whole course of our obedience.

This must suffice for the first branch of our query: whether a man may not obey God in reference to God's bestowing of outward mercies and enjoyments here and now. In a word, it seems more agreeable to the Gospel, and to the frame of a Christian soul, to say that we ought to obey God upon the knowledge, the belief, and the persuasion that God will bless us and that He will withhold no good thing from us, than to say that we are to obey God that we may gain good temporal things by our obedience. I shall prosecute this matter no further. If, in that which I have written, I have differed from others, it is not in disrespect to others whose judgments I respect, and I hope they will make allowance for me if I have dissented from their opinions on reasonable grounds.

With reference to spiritual benefits

We now proceed to the second main branch of the query propounded: Whether we are to do duties with reference and respect to the obtaining of spiritual good things. Some divines say that we are not to suggest any respects or ends at all in the doing of duty. They not only exclude base ends, carnal purposes, and secular advantages, but they exclude also the highest and noblest ends. They tell us plainly that we are not to humble ourselves, fast, and pray, for the prevention of any evil, or the procuring of any good. Nay, they go yet higher and say that we are not to do duty with respect to the obtaining of any spiritual good, such as pardon, peace, joy, assurance, the light of God's countenance, the subduing of lusts, and all else. In so saying, such men propound an irrational opinion which strips men of their reason (for if you take away the end which every reasonable creature, as a reasonable creature, proposes to himself in his actions, you bring man down to the level of the beasts). Yet such men, that they may seem to be reasonable in their paradox, give us two grounds for it:

1. They tell us that we must not think that we can purchase by our prayers and duties that which has been purchased already for us by Christ. Christ, they say, has fully purchased all that we need – pardon, peace, joy, and all good. Therefore no more is required.

2. They tell us further that all spiritual blessings are sufficiently provided for us in Christ, and that God has decreed all good things for us in Christ. Therefore we must not think that we can get them by our prayers.

These are the two reasons on which (may I say it without offence?) this unreasonable and destructive opinion seems to be founded.

Certainly I need not say much against this opinion, for if it be but twice repeated, it will be as good as a confutation of it. Indeed, if this opinion be a truth, we must have another Bible to countenance it. What do we read of more frequently than this: 'Call upon me in the day of trouble, and I will deliver thee' (Ps. 50.15); 'Ask, and it shall be given you; seek, and ye shall find; knock, and it shall be opened unto you' (Luke 11.9)? Does not the apostle desire them to pray for him? and for what end? He tells them – 'that utterance may be given unto me, that I may open my mouth boldly, to make known the mystery of the Gospel' (Eph. 6.19). Does he not ask another church to pray that he may be delivered from unreasonable and wicked men? (2 Thess. 3.2). Does not James bid us, if we be sick, to send for the elders of the church : and why? To pray for us. And why pray? That we may be healed! 'Pray for one another, that ye may be healed' (James 5.16).

But I am weary of this contention. In almost every place in Scripture where a duty is commanded, there is an end propounded. And what can be more destructive to grace and to reason than such an opinion? It would be no more absurd to reason, to say that we must not eat to satisfy our hunger, drink to satisfy our thirst, feed to nourish ourselves, but that we are to feed out of mere instinct, as do the beasts, not from reasonable motives as men. But what? are we to do duty for no reason at all? May we not confess sin that we may be humbled and made sensible of it? May we not hear the Word that our understandings may be bettered, our affections quickened, our faith strengthened? Surely the objectors propound these ends in their own preaching, otherwise why do they go to so much pains to persuade (I do not say convince) men's understandings that they are in error? And may we not use ordinances for the increase of our graces, and for the abatement and weakening of our corruptions? And may we not do works of charity to refresh the poor? May we not relieve those who are in extremities? And are not these ends? And is it not the same with other duties?

But if all this should be denied, yet this much will be agreed, we hope, that we may do duty and walk in the ways of obedience, to adorn our profession, to dignify the Gospel, to glorify God, to benefit the saints, and to win others. And are not these ends? And were not these as much purchased by Christ, and provided for by God, as the other? Sure it is that, much as we have need of God, so much the more has God no need of us. His glory, His Gospel, His cause does not depend upon us. God could advance this, and maintain the other, without us. And therefore, how little of men, how little of God, how little of reason, how little of Scripture there is in such a tenet, I leave to all to judge.

But yet, that their show of reason may not go without an answer, I shall say one further word to them. It is this:

Although Christ has purchased all good things for us, yet it pleased God to bestow them in a way of seeking. We see this in Ezek. 36.37 (which follows upon the most free and absolute promises): 'I will yet for this be inquired of by the house of Israel, to do it for them'. God promised to bestow the blessings, and promised (like Himself) to grant all freely without any respect to man's deserts, as He tells them in verse 32: 'Not for your sakes do I this, saith the Lord God, be it known unto you'. No! It was for His own Name's sake. And yet He tells them in the words just quoted: 'I will yet for this be enquired of by the house of Israel to do it for them'. All this plainly shows that, though God had promised, and promised freely, to bestow these things on them, yet He would bestow them in a way of seeking.

We say yet again, that though God will bestow good things in a way of believing and praying, yet they are not the purchase of our prayers, but the gift of His own mercy. And I appeal to all, whether they have ever heard any conscientious minister of the Gospel to say that prayer was the meriting cause of any mercy? Did ever any say that duty came in as an influential cause for the granting of any mercy? Has it not always been shown as a subservient means, not as a procuring cause, of any mercy from God? When God has a purpose to give, He stirs up the heart to seek, and this stirring up of the heart to seek is an evidence that He has a purpose to bestow. He loves to bestow His mercy in a way of seeking, that we may be encouraged to come to Him, and to regard our blessings as the fruits of prayer and the performance by God of His promises to us.

But perhaps it will be said: If these blessings are freely promised, why is there a condition attached to the bestowing of them? I answer thus: Some there are that say that, though God's promises are free in respect of the making of them, yet they are conditional in respect of the performance of them. Though they are made from sheer mercy, yet God fulfils them in relation to the performance of our subservient duty. If we do but add to this the truth that the subservient condition or duty which is prerequisite to the performance of the promise, is nothing of our bringing but first of God's bestowing, I do not see how this statement in any way detracts from the freedom of God's grace either in the making or the performing of the promise.

To take an instance: God tells us that He will give to him that is athirst (Rev. 21.6). Here is a condition or qualification. Yet this does not take away from the freeness of grace. Notwithstanding this qualification, God tells us that He gives to him that is athirst, and what can be freer than a gift? As has been said, God gives both the grace of desiring, and the grace desired. 'Gift' implies freeness of grace. But some may still object and say that it cannot be a gift if God requires thirst. This qualification, they say, implies it to be no gift of grace. To set this aside, God has been pleased to add to the former word 'gift' this other word 'freely'. 'I will *give* to him that is athirst of the fountain of the water of life *freely*.' Thus it is clear that grace is found here in all its plenitude. That which God requires as subservient to the promise is not of our bringing, till first of God's bestowing; not of our purchasing, but of God's giving. God has engaged Himself by covenant, not only to give the promise, but to give also whatever is required as necessary and subservient to the promise. If indeed there had been anything required which was of our bringing and which was not first of all of God's bestowing, it would have gone contrary to grace and would have altered the nature of the thing. It would have made that to be man's by purchase which was of God's gift, even though what we brought bore no proportion to that which God gave. If so much as one penny is required of us for the purchase of a kingdom, though this falls infinitely short of the true worth of the kingdom, yet this alters the nature of the thing, and makes that a purchase which without that would be a gift. So here. If any thing is required of us which is not of God's giving and bestowing, though the thing required of us were never so small, yet it would alter the nature of the gift and make grace to be no grace. But when that which is of our bringing is truly of God's bestowing and giving, the nature of the gift remains, and there is no infringement upon the freeness of grace. If God requires faith in a man to close with the promise, and gives him the faith to close with the promise, certainly this is no prejudice to grace. The prophet Isaiah says: 'In the Lord have I righteousness and strength' (45.24) – righteousness to those that believe on Him, and strength to enable them to come to Him. As the sea sends out waters to fetch us to it, so God sends out strength from Himself to draw us to Himself. And so all is of grace, which can no way be grace, if it be not every way truly grace.

And if promises of grace, though absolute and free in themselves, yet are conditional in respect of their fulfilment, much more may I say this of promises of comfort, peace, and joy. If this were but acknowledged, men certainly would not run upon these rocks, that a believer immediately following upon an act of sin, may take comfort and hear God speaking peace in the promise. It is claimed that he may then hear all the gracious language of heaven, as though he had not sinned. It is the failure of men to see that, in a certain way, promises are conditional, that inevitably carries men on such rocks as these. Yet I say, and say again, that these promises are conditional in respect of their fulfilment, whatever they are in their own nature. It is for this reason that we do duties as subservient means for the bringing about of their fulfilment. Not that duty is the cause of their fulfilment, or that it has any causal influence leading to fulfilment, but that it is the subservient means for the obtaining of the things which God has freely promised. God has promised these things to His people, and this is the way in which He will fulfil them, as he tells us: 'He meeteth him that rejoiceth and worketh righteousness' (Isa. 64.5). And again: 'To him, that ordereth his conversation aright will I show the salvation of God' (Ps. 50.23). And again: 'As many as walk according to this rule, peace be on them' (Gal. 6.16). Thus we see that the way in which God performs these promises is in a way of duty and obedience. And therefore may we do duty with respect to the enjoyment of the promises.

But there is a further objection which must be answered. Some men will say that that which is the fruit of grace and justification cannot be a condition preceding grace and justification; but to perform duty acceptably is a consequence of our justification and the work of grace in us; it cannot therefore be said to be a precedent condition.

All our learned and holy writers, speaking against the Papists in their treatises against justification by works, are agreed that the acceptable performance of duty by the godly is a fruit of their justification. For instance, Augustine says, 'Good works follow justification; they do not precede justification'; and again he says, 'While we see good works wrought by men, we see faith wrought in men.' Among other arguments against the Papists, this appears. If we are justified before we can work, then we are not justified by our works. But we are so justified; therefore we cannot be justified by our works. That we are justified before we can work, the Scripture sets forth plainly. It tells us that without Christ we can do nothing, and that we are created in Christ Jesus unto good works (Eph. 2.10): that in ourselves we are but dead men, that all our life is from Christ, and that we can have no life from Christ until we have union with him: for 'he that hath the Son hath life, and he that hath not the Son of God hath not life' (1 John 5.12). And as soon as there is life and union there is justification, for the gift of life and the justification are simultaneous, though in order of nature one may be conceived before the other. It has been rightly said: 'Let us work from justification, not for justification.'

It will be said, however, that if this argument is true which we thus oppose to the teachings of the Papists, that we must not work that we may be justified, but must be justified that we may work, then the performance of duties cannot be said to be the preceding condition for receiving blessing, seeing that the blessings are the subsequent fruits of grace and justification. Thus have I raised this objection to the utmost height I can, and presented it in the best light. And at this height I had thought to have dealt with it. But I find that it leads into many intricate questions which are fitter for discussion in a separate treatise rather than dealt with here. But if better and more able hands do not undertake it (it is my earnest desire that they may), then possibly God may afford opportunity to me, one who is the most unworthy of those that labour in the Gospel, to speak something on such a subject as this. In the meantime I shall propound a few things for serious and thorough consideration :

First, Is it not possible that the conditions for blessing which have been considered are both conditions that precede blessing and also the subsequent fruits of grace? This will especially appear if we look upon them as conditions of God's bestowing before anything of ourselves enters into them so as to make them appear to be qualifications for grace. May they not be qualifications which we receive from grace, and indeed grace in themselves, presupposing the existence of faith?

Secondly, We should inquire whether it is possible to draw good and safe distinctions between the qualifications in or by which a soul comes to Christ (namely, a sense of need, hunger and thirst, and spiritual poverty: Matt. 11.28 and 5.3–6) and the qualification, namely faith, which actually brings the soul to Christ. And is it possible to call the first the qualifications of grace, and the second the qualifications to grace, especially if it be admitted that these qualifications to grace are not of man, though in man?

Thirdly, Let us inquire whether there are not some works

in preparation for grace which may be said to be *from* the Spirit but yet are not *with* the Spirit; that is, which proceed from the Spirit of sanctification, and yet they are not *with* the sanctifying Spirit: even as the light of the morning is from the sun, yet not with the sun.

Fourthly, We should inquire whether it is or is not true that Christ comes not to us before He comes into us. Have we some kind of life from Christ before we come to live in Christ or Christ comes to live in us?

Fifthly, We should inquire whether we may rightly draw distinctions between active and passive preparations for receiving life in Christ. May we rightly understand as 'passive' preparations the emptying us of sin and self by the Spirit of God? and as 'active' preparations the begetting in us of desires and hungerings and thirstings after Christ by the same Spirit? And do both kinds of preparation presuppose the existence of faith and of Christ in the soul? Has Christ entered the soul, as light enters into a dark room, dispelling rather than expelling the darkness, driving out the darkness by His entrance rather than throwing out darkness before He enters?

Sixthly, We should also consider whether certain learned men, in speaking of the passive and active reception of Christ by the soul, have thereby drawn a safe distinction; also whether in the one case the soul receives Christ as a dead man receives life, in the other, as a living man receives food; also whether the one may be called the soul's interest in Christ and the other the manifestation of that interest. If these things are so, it may further be considered whether many of those things which are said to be preparations for the reception of Christ by the soul do not actually presuppose Christ to be already in us, and do not precede the soul's interest in Him, though they do precede the manifestation of that interest.

Seventhly, It is to be considered whether the order of God's working may not differ from that which is to be our order of preaching, and whether we should not make some use of the distinction between God's ordinary and His extraordinary methods of working in the hearts and lives of men.

Eighthly, It is worthy of consideration whether, for the same reason that all preparations (the preceding work and acts of God in the soul of man, for example, conviction of sin and the revelation of Christ) leading to justification are denied, the fact that faith itself precedes justification may be denied also. For if so, then certainly both 'faith' and 'justification' will have to be taken in another sense than Scripture seems to give them, and long usage has accorded them.

Therefore it would be also worth our pains to give some thought to the determination of the true nature of faith and justification, and also to ask ourselves what is the nature of faith. Is faith actually and truly the instrument of justification, or only the evidence that we are justified? Does faith truly give us an interest in Christ, or does it merely give us the manifestation that we have such an interest? Certain other questions will help us in this inquiry, as, for example, whether the faith which justifies a man is an act of recumbency, that is to say, a resting on Christ for the soul's interest, or whether it is rather a persuasion and assurance that the soul already has an interest in Him. Certain Scriptures which bear on this subject should be well weighed, chiefly Rom. 3.28 : 'We conclude that a man is justified by faith without the deeds of the law', and Rom. 5.1 : 'Therefore being justified by faith, we have peace with God through our Lord Jesus Christ'.

As for justification itself, such considerations would show whether it is an act of God entirely external to the person justified, or whether it is His immanent act; whether it is an act of God in time, or whether that which is done in time is improperly called justification, but is merely the manifestation to a man of what God has done for him from all eternity. As for those who are of the latter opinion, they should inquire whether, for the elucidation of this truth, it might not be admitted that a distinction should be drawn between the several stages of justification. Thus we may be said to be justified in God's decree, in which sense we are justified from eternity. Again, we are justified meritoriously in the death of Christ who laid down at His death the full price for the payment of our debt. Again, it may be said that we are actually justified when we come to believe. And once more, we are justified in the court of our own conscience, and thus justified to ourselves, when we come to assurance. And there is one further stage: we are perfectly justified when we are glorified, that is, when Christ shall present His spouse without spot, or wrinkle, or any such thing, when the church shall be all fair and without spot or sin. If these things are not admitted, the order observed in Scripture will seem to be inverted, and we shall run from God's revealed will to God's secret will. Yea, and a man may stand actually justified according to this opinion, while he stands truly and actually under the power, the reign, and the rage of Satan and sin.

These things I have brought forward with the suggestion that they need consideration. It was from such considerations that I had intended to answer the various objections to my doctrine. But I find that they demand (as I have already intimated) a separate treatise from me, unless better hands than mine (as I desire) engage in the work.

For the present, I say no more than this, that those dispositions and qualifications which are prerequisites to blessing, in no way rob God's grace of its freeness, for they are themselves the results of His grace. They are of God's bestowing, not of our purchasing; they are not of our bringing, apart from God's first giving. We say that no qualifications on man's part from man are required, though there is something required on man's part from God. Do those who deny the need for preparation in the heart of man for the receiving of Christ also deny the necessity of the means of grace to those not yet brought to Christ?

If preparations in man's heart are not necessary, then the

means of grace are not necessary to such men. But the means of grace are necessary. It is said that faith comes by hearing (Rom. 10.17), and, if the means are not necessary, then men may believe and be justified before ever they have heard of Christ. Yet I know that this consequence of the error will be denied.

Consider this: If by the means of grace God prepares the soul for coming to Christ, then take away the need for preparations for coming to Christ, and you take away the necessity for the means of grace. But it is certain that, by the means of grace, God prepares men for coming to Christ. By these means of grace He reveals to men their state of misery; through them he causes them to see their sinfulness and need of Christ. In them He shows how Christ and the promises meet their need, and kindle in their souls a desire and thirst after Him and earnest longings for Him. This is to them the morning of grace, the dawnings of faith and conversion, and as such they are the harbingers of Christ.

It is said of John the Baptist, who was the 'prodromus' (forerunner or harbinger) of Christ, both of His coming into the world and also into the heart, that he was to make ready, or prepare, a people for the Lord (Luke 1.17). How did he do this but by his ministry? Christ will have some one to go before Him to prepare for His entrance. It is said of the seventy disciples whom Christ sent out to preach, that He sent them 'to every city and place whither he himself would come'. And wherefore did He send them before Him, but to prepare men's hearts for the receiving of Christ when the Sent One actually came to them. This is seen in the text which He gave the seventy to preach from: 'Go and say unto them, the kingdom of God is come nigh unto you' (Luke 10.9). It is with Christ in His entrance into the soul as it is with a prince's coming to a place. The prince has his harbingers who go before him, his court or such as go with him, and his attendants, or such as are his followers and come after him. It is so with

Christ. The harbingers of Christ are those preparatory work-ings – conviction of sin, the hearing of Christ and the prom-ises, the earnest longings, the thirsting and the seeking after Him. Christ's court consists of all the graces of His Spirit which He works in His first entrance into the soul. And His attendants or followers are the peace that passes all under-standing (Phil. 4.7), and the joy which is unspeakable and glorious in the Holy Ghost (1 Pet. 1.8). It is possible for Christ to enter the house before His followers come in. There may be faith without assurance and grace without joy. There can be no true joy without grace, but there may be true grace with-out joy.

But I will proceed no further with this theme. This must suffice for the second branch of this query.

With reference to eternal rewards

The third and last query runs thus: Whether we may obey and do duty to God with respect to eternal rewards. Those who deny this, do so upon two grounds. Some say that Christ has purchased, and God has fully provided Heaven and glory for us. Therefore we are not to have any respect to it in our obedience.

I agree that we are not to have respect to the purchasing of eternal rewards by our obedience, but we may have respect to the possession of them in our obedience. We may have respect to the enjoyment of them in our obedience, though not to the obtaining of them by our obedience. To have an eye to our enjoyment of the rewards in our obedience is one thing, and to have an eye to the obtaining of it by our obedience is quite another. Certainly, those who preach obedience and holiness do not preach them as the cause, but as the way. They tell us of the necessity for them, not in regard to the claims of jus-tice but in respect of God's requirement that we must be made meet for the inheritance of the saints in light (Col. 1.12). As

Bernard says : 'Good works are the way to the reward, not the cause of the reward.'

Good works are necessary, not in respect of causality, but in respect of God's order and means and ordination. 'He hath called us to virtue and glory', says the apostle (2 Pet. 1.3) – to virtue as the preparation, to glory as the fruition. In respect of God's requirements here and now, we say that works of righteousness and holiness must be forthcoming, for certainly God makes none happy hereafter but those whom He makes holy here, He brings none to glory but those in whom He works grace. 'He gives grace and glory' (Ps. 84.11). He brings heaven into the soul before He brings the soul to heaven.

But if it be claimed that good works are to satisfy justice and to win Heaven and glory for us, we cry them down, and say with the apostle : 'Not by works of righteousness which we have done, but according to his mercy he saved us' (Tit. 3.5). Let this saying be ever in your ears : Do all righteousness, but learn to rest in none; be in duty in respect of performance, but out of duty and in Christ in respect of dependence. This will suffice for answer to those who deny duty with respect to reward for the first of the reasons stated.

There are other persons who deny that we are to have respect to these eternal rewards in our obedience, but it is upon another ground. They assert that it savours not of an ingenuous Gospel spirit, but rather of a mercenary and servile spirit. They say we are to serve God even were there no heaven, no hell, no rewards, no punishments. To illustrate this, I mention the alleged story of a woman who carried fire in one hand and water in the other. Another met her who inquired what she intended to do with her two burdens. She answered : With this water I will quench all the fires of hell, and with this fire I will burn up all the joys of heaven, that I may serve God neither for fear of punishment nor for hope of reward, but purely and solely for Himself. She showed good affections, but it will appear in what I have further to say that she lacked clear perceptions of Heaven and glory. If she had conceived of that glory aright, she would not have spoken after this fashion; for there is nothing in Heaven that a glorified soul needs to part with; there is nothing there which needs to be burned up; there is nothing there but God in grace and glory, as I shall explain shortly.

There is another opinion which some express, which is that a godly man may perform duties and walk in the way of obedience with a respect to the recompense of the reward. But this opinion is so modified, so tempered and allayed, that it is a wonder that any should take offence at it. It suggests that, though we may have respect to Heaven and glory and our salvation, yet these must not be the supreme and primary respects, but only secondary and inferior. Also, they must not be held singly and solely, but conjunctively and jointly with God's glory; not absolutely, but subordinately to that glory.

It is the saying of a former saint : 'Not Heaven, O Lord, but God and Christ. Rather ten thousand times Christ without Heaven, than Heaven without Christ. But seeing that Thou hast joined them together, so that I cannot enjoy one without the other, then give me both, O Lord; but not Christ for Heaven, but Heaven, O Lord, for Christ.' And Augustine has said : 'He loves Thee not, O Lord, who loves something before Thee, which he loves not on account of Thee.'

It is certainly true that Heaven and glory are not to be either the sole or the supreme grounds and ends of our obedience, though we look to them to enliven us in our way and in our movements. They are not to be the reason for our moving. We should regard them as refreshments in the way, but not as the reason why we undertake our journey. The apostle's expression may serve to indicate this to us : 'He had respect to the recompense of the reward' (Heb. 11.26). The Greek is not 'blepo' (to look), but 'apoblepo' (to look from or out from). He 'cast an eye' when he was on his journey, to cheer him in his way and give him encouragement, lest he should think of the great things he had refused and lest the flesh should begin to tell him that he had made a hard bargain. For this reason he steals a look from glory; he turns to his cordial; he casts an eye to the recompense of the reward. By this means he renews his strength and gets new and fresh encouragement to continue his journey. He does not make this a reason why he undertakes the journey, but only a means of quickening him in his way. It is not the mainspring of his motion, but the oil to the wheels so that he may move the more cheerfully.

Some there are who distinguish between young beginners and grown Christians. At the first entrance of the soul into the ways of grace, they say, a man looks upon heaven and hell, the one to drive him out of sin, the other to persuade and draw him into the ways of holiness. But when once a soul has truly entered upon the ways of life, he finds so much sweetness in God and His ways, that now he serves God with a more free and ingenuous spirit. As the Samaritans said, 'Now we believe, not because of thy saying: for we have heard him ourselves, and know that this is indeed the Christ, the Saviour of the world' (John 4.41–42). In a similar way it is said, 'Now we serve Thee, not for fear of punishment, nor for hope of reward, but because we see such beauty in Thyself, such sweetness in Thy ways, that if there were no other heaven, then this were heaven enough.'

The case of the prodigal seems to support this argument (Luke 15). When first he was awakened and convinced of his sin and misery, he said, 'I will arise and go to my father, and say unto him, Father, I have sinned against heaven and in thy sight and am no more worthy to be called thy son; make me as one of thy hired servants.' He desired to be a hired servant. But later, when he came to his father, and saw his mercy and indulgence, how he ran to meet him and embraced him, he ceases to talk of being a hired servant. He was now overcome with love, and therefore he only remembers the wickedness he has done, and abhors himself for it, saying, 'Father, I have sinned against heaven and before thee'. He mentions hired servants no more.

Thus, too it is with the soul of the believer. When he is first awakened to see sin, and misery by sin, he says, 'O make me as one of thy hired servants.' Fear of hell and desire of heaven are his two great springs of action. But when once the man comes over to Christ and the promise, when once he has tasted of God's mercy in pardoning him and God's goodness in receiving him, then he falls down and abhors himself, as it is said happened to those upon whom God settled the promises (see Ezek. 36.31). And now all he desires is to serve God for Himself. He sees so much beauty in Him, He has tasted so much mercy shown by Him, that if he had the strength of an angel, it were all too little to be laid out for Him. Nothing that is his – the blood in his veins, the life that surges through his limbs, his soul, his spirit – is too dear to be spared from His service. The only question now is, not, what will God give me? but, what can I give God? What shall I render to the Lord for all His goodness? The man is willing to go through a sea and through a wilderness, through any difficulties and any duties. All that he can do falls infinitely short of what his heart and good will would render to God. All his expressions fall short of his enlarged affections. And though God should do no more for him, yet his heart burns with such affection for God that he counts all he can do for Him but a small part of that which he would wish to do.

In answer then to this third part of our query as to whether a Christian man may not do duty with an eye to the recompense of the reward, that is, with an eye to Heaven and glory, I answer affirmatively, and in opposition to the contrary opinion, I shall state and prove the two following propositions: (1) that we may obey God with respect to heaven and glory, (2) that we ought to have respect to heaven and glory in our obedience. I shall endeavour to establish these two propositions, though not upon the grounds on which the law-fulness of eyeing rewards in our obedience is usually based. I shall labour to establish it on such spiritual and true grounds as shall show wherein I differ from the arguments directed against it in the previous part of our inquiry.

Proposition 1: That it is lawful for Christians to obey God with respect to eternal rewards – heaven and glory

In looking into this question I find that those who have main-tained the contrary opinion have based that opinion upon false conceptions of heaven and glory. Their thoughts about heaven have been too low and too carnal by far. Probably these low thoughts have arisen from the consideration that they must have no eye to heaven in their obedience. I have already dealt with the meaning of 'eyeing the reward', so can at once pro-ceed to explain what is truly meant by heaven and glory.

If we take away or separate that from Heaven which a carnal heart conceives to be heaven, then that which remains is heaven to a godly man. Carnal men fancy heaven under carnal notions. They look upon it as a place where there is freedom from all misery, and where there is a fulness of all pleasures and happiness. But both these – the pleasures and the happiness, the freedom and enjoyment – they fancy in a way which complies with the carnality of their natural hearts. This indeed is a Turkish heaven, but it is not a Christian's heaven. Certainly we have heaven described in sumptuous terms in the Scriptures (Rev. 21.18–19). The walls are of jasper, the city is pure gold, the foundations are garnished with all kinds of precious stones, the first foundation is of jasper . . . and the twelve gates are twelve pearls. Thus is God pleased to pencil it out, as if He would tempt a world-ling, and even corrupt sense itself which shall never come there, to seek the enjoyment of it.

It must be well understood that this is spoken by way of metaphor, because the glory of heaven cannot be pencilled out as it really is. Therefore God descends to our weakness and even to sense itself, and describes heaven and glory by such things as are known to men to be precious. Not that we are to conceive that heaven is any such thing, or that there is any such thing in heaven. If a man thinks so, I shall spoil his heaven before I have done.

God has no need to be indebted to stones, even precious stones, to make heaven glorious any more than the sun has any need to be indebted to the stars to make the day. God Himself fills heaven with glory and makes it infinitely glorious. God in heaven is the glory of heaven.

For what purpose are such poor beggarly things of the senses needed in heaven by those who are all spirit and glory? These things are below the spirit of a godly man while he is in the earth. He has a more noble spirit than to set much value on them here. He can trample on gold and silver, pearls and diamonds. And if his spirit is above these things here, what are these to him in heaven? If these are below him while he is here below, what are they then when he gets above? These are but beggarly glory compared with the meanest glory in heaven. Everywhere a Christian turns his eyes in Heaven will reveal a far greater glory than these are. Every glorified soul shall be more glorious than the sun in its glory. Alas, what are precious stones but mere pebble stones as compared to the glory of a glorified saint!

I conceive, then, that by eternal rewards is meant whatever ought to be the utmost of the desire of a renewed and sancti-fied soul. Certain other writers have written about this matter excellently, so that I need not enlarge further. It is, in brief, the fruition and enjoyment of God; the enjoyment of Christ, who is the Pearl of great price; the enjoyment of the Spirit, the true Comforter; it is the perfection and fulness of grace; it is an eternal Sabbath, a rest, a rest in Jehovah, in whom there is all rest. It is a rest after pilgrimage. All pantings after Him here below are now exchanged for rests in Him. He is the

Christian's centre, his proper place of rest. It is a glorious rest. Here rest and glory seldom meet; in Heaven they meet perfectly, and that for all eternity.

Does it not then seem that a Christian may truly desire all this? May he not eye it all, and have respect to it all in his service and obedience?

May we not desire and have regard to the enjoyment of God in our service? David could say, 'Whom have I in heaven but thee? and there is none upon earth that I desire beside thee' (Ps. 73.25). The enjoyment of God was the utmost of his desire in heaven, and it is recorded as the highest privilege a Christian can enjoy through Christ, to be brought by Him to God (1 Pet. 3.18). And may we not take it into our consideration here below? Certainly the more respect we have to the enjoyment of God in our obedience, the more noble is our obedience. The more we give attention to the enjoyment of God while we are engaged in duty, the more noble are our spirits in duty. And in prayer and the doing of duty, may we not hope to get a little communion with God and Christ as we engage in them? Without such regard, our duties are not sound. And is it not right to serve God, and in that service to have respect to the full enjoyment and communion with Him which are known in heaven? To hold a contrary view of this matter is absurd.

And may we not have regard to the enjoyment of Christ as we follow after God and Christ in the ways of holiness? Not indeed that we may purchase Him by our obedience, but that we may journey to Him in our obedience; yea, and walk in ways of service with the hope that therein we may enjoy Him; not as the merit of our service, but as the purpose in our serving.

Further, may we not also desire the Spirit of God, who is the only Comforter? And may we not serve God with regard to the enjoyment of Him who comforts and sanctifies us? He is now in us, and hereafter we shall be in Him. This is the preoccupation of glory, even as it was experienced by John who said, 'I was in the Spirit on the Lord's day' (Rev. 1.10).

And may we not obey God and serve Him with respect to perfection and fulness of grace yet to come to us? If we serve Him here with an eye to the additions of grace which He sends us, may we not obey Him with respect to the fulness of grace yet to be bestowed? Is it right for us to pray now, to walk in the use of ordinances and in all the ways of duty, trusting that thereby we may get a little more grace, a little more faith, more love, more brokenness of heart? If so, how much more may we serve God and obey Him with respect to the fulness and perfection of grace in a coming day! This is that which we breathe after, and pray for, and hope for, even perfection and full satisfaction. 'When I awake', says David, 'I shall be satisfied with thy likeness' (Ps. 17.15). And certainly, that which is the saints' satisfaction hereafter is the saints' desire here. That which they breathe after in all their service as their satisfaction, may be respected and eyed here as our duty in all our service. If those duties are not well done in which we have not sought after communion with God and Christ, and also the growth of our grace, in the performance of them, then surely we not only may, but it is our duty to eye these things and to have respect to them in our service and obedience.

Further, may we not live in the hope of a perfect Sabbath while we are doing duty? What is it but a rest? Is not rest the end of all labour? Does not labour tend to rest? And is not this a rest, a rest from sin, a rest in God, a rest with praise and admiring and glorifying of God to all eternity? And may we not labour in the hope and expectation of reaching this rest? May we not do service with an eye to the obtaining of such a Sabbath? There shall we rest for ever, and never, never sin. We shall rest in service, we shall rest in God. 'Even for this cause we labour and faint not' (2 Cor. 4.16).

Tell me now, after this little that has been said, whether we may not serve God with respect to eternal rewards? May not a Christian serve God with respect to these things? Nay, is he a Christian at all who does not have regard to these promised blessings in his service? Why, what is salvation, what is heaven, what is glory, but all this? I wonder what forethought a person has of heaven and what he thinks of glory and salvation, when he says that we are not to eye these things, nor to have respect to them in our obedience. Certainly he thinks of them under false notions. His thoughts are not God's thoughts. He looks upon them as the world does, carnally, not spiritually. None will own that heaven as his happiness which he may not have respect to in his service; nay, which he does not make his ambition and his aim in his service. The apostle seems to imply as much as this in 2 Cor. 4.18: 'We look not at the things which are seen, but at the things which are not seen'. This implies that we make the things which are not seen our ambition and aim. And if so, then certainly we may have respect to them. Let us be ashamed to imagine that to be heaven which a godly man may not be permitted to eye, and have respect to, in his obedience; nay, make his ambition and end in obeying; that is, not so much that heaven which comes to us from God, as that heaven which lies in God. If we speak of heaven in an abstract way, it is but a notion. This can never make a man happy. But if we speak of heaven as the place where we shall be with God and find our full salvation in God, then as heaven becomes our happiness so also it becomes our holiness. And to this we must have an eye in all our obedience. In this way poor Christians may overcome those doubts which are usually the results of a jealous misgiving spirit.

But even so, there may be some Christians who labour under further difficulties. Ah, someone will say, I fear that my service is hypocritical and out of self-love, for I aim at myself. I do service with respect to Heaven and glory. I answer thus: We never read that God charged any believer with hypocrisy who had respect to the world to come. Indeed, He has charged those who have had respect to this present world, and to earthly things; as He said to the Israelites: 'You have not fasted and prayed to me; you assembled together for corn and wine and oil' (see Hosea 7.14). But He never charged any soul with double-mindedness who had an eye and respect to heaven and glory.

I say again, conceive of heaven under the right notion; get right thoughts of heaven; look upon heaven as I have set it forth; make that your Heaven which I have proved to be a Christian's heaven, and then you may carry an eye and respect to it in all your obedience. Nay, the more eye and respect you have for heaven thus described, the more spiritual and heavenly you will be. In this you do not aim at pleasing your corrupt self, but aiding your best self; not yourself in opposition to God, or separated from God, but yourself in God. You lose yourself in Him, to find yourself in Him when you are swallowed up in His likeness.

But some Christians are troubled by another scruple. They say, I fear that my desires are not true, for I do not desire grace for its own sake but grace for glory, grace for heaven. I answer as before: Conceive aright of heaven. Do not look upon it with a carnal eye, as a place of freedom from the miseries you feel and as a place of enjoyment of the happiness and pleasures you hope for. But look upon it as a place where you will have communion with God, enjoyment of Christ, perfection and fulness of grace, freedom from all sin and corruption and spiritual imperfection. Do this, and you do not sin in desiring grace for heaven. If you look upon grace and heaven as two different things, you may err in desiring grace for heaven. But if you look upon heaven as the fulness of grace, then you may desire grace for heaven. You may desire grace here as the beginning of heaven, as the earnest of glory, and as that which will entitle you to perfection and fulness of glory hereafter.

In brief, then, he who desires grace merely for glory, and looks upon that glory as a thing quite different from grace, has desires which are not right. But you may desire grace with respect to heaven so long as you desire heaven with respect to grace. The more enlarged you are in such desires, the more gracious and spiritual are your principles. The position has been well summed up by one author in the words: 'Sanctification is glory in the bud; glory is sanctification in the flower.'

Proposition 2: Christians not only may have but ought to have respect to heaven and glory in their obedience.

I come next to show that Christians not only may have, but ought to have, respect to heaven and glory in their obedience. It is not only 'may' but 'must'. You may obey God with respect to heaven, but you must respect heaven in your obedience. It is that which God has urged upon us to fortify our hearts against the fear of earth's troubles, and to bear up our hearts under the sense of any calamities. It is to be noticed that when Christ desired to arm His disciples against all the fears and evils they might encounter in this life, He draws the encouragement from the truth that God intends to give them a kingdom: 'Fear not, little flock, for it is your Father's good pleasure to give you the kingdom' (Luke 12.32). He brings the harbour into the sea, the rest into the labour, the glory into the trouble; and this encourages a soul to go through all. If we do not pay any respect to this source of encouragement, we slight the Lord's own word. As it is a sin to slight the consolations of God (Job 15.11), so it is no less a sin to make light of the encouragements of God. God gives us these in order to help faith against sense, to furnish faith with arguments against the carnal reasonings of the flesh, and to strengthen us in the greatest straits and distresses the world can bring upon us.

The saints have been helped thus in their fiercest battles. We have already seen how Moses was thus helped to suffer affliction with the people of God. Did he not look for the recompense of the reward? That glory and happiness to come, which was made real and visible to him in this present world, encouraged him to slight all the greatness of Egypt. It rendered all treasures of earth too little for his spirit, and his spirit too big to be daunted by the world's discouragements.

It was the same with the apostle Paul. He was troubled on every side, but he laboured and he did not faint: wherefore? Because (as he said) 'our light affliction which is but for a moment worketh for us a far more exceeding and eternal weight of glory, while we look, not at the things which are seen, but at the things which are not seen' (2 Cor. 4.17–18). We thus see where the apostle obtained his strength and encouragement to go through all his troubles and distresses. He looked above those things which are seen, and considered those things which are not seen.

To be brief: would you walk thankfully and cheerfully? Would you be strong to do and to suffer? Would you submit to all God's disposings? Would you rejoice in your sufferings? If you would do these things, you must have an eye for the recompense of the reward. I will speak briefly of each in turn.

Would you walk thankfully? The right consideration of the matter will make us burst out into praises in our lowest conditions. Here is matter enough for praises. Hear the apostle as he bursts into praise: 'Blessed be the God and Father of our Lord Jesus Christ, which according to his abundant mercy hath begotten us again unto a lively hope . . . to an inheritance incorruptible, and undefiled and that fadeth not away, reserved in heaven for you' (1 Peter 1.3). Indeed such thoughts and considerations will fill us full of heaven and glory, and make us break forth into songs of thanksgiving for His great goodness: 'Who hath made us meet to be partakers of the inheritance of the saints in light' (Col. 1.12).

Would you walk cheerfully? Would you be filled with joy and comfort in the midst of all your sad conditions? Would you joy in tribulations? Then consider the things of the Heaven to which you are moving: 'They took joyfully the spoiling of their goods, knowing in themselves that they had in heaven a better and an enduring substance' (Heb. 10.34). It is reported of Caesar, that when he was sad, he used to say to himself, 'Think that thou art Caesar.' If Caesar thought that his earthly greatness was enough to bear up his heart in any trouble, how much more should the consideration of the great things reserved for us cheer our hearts and comfort our spirits, no matter how sad our condition! He that lives much in the thoughts of heaven, lives much the life of heaven, that is to say, thankfully and cheerfully.

The philosophers say that if men lived above the second region of the atmosphere they would live above all storms, for there is nothing found there but serenity and clearness. It is true of those souls who can live in heaven that they have rest in labour, calm amid storms, tranquillity in tempests, and comforts amidst their greatest distresses.

Would you be strong to do the will of God? The same considerations will give you strength and encouragement. The apostle brings in this as an encouragement: 'Whatsoever ye do, do it heartily . . . knowing that of the Lord ye shall receive the reward of the inheritance' (Col. 3.23–24). Likewise, in 1 Cor. 15.58: 'Be always abounding in the work of the Lord, forasmuch as ye know that your labour is not in vain in the Lord.' You may read similar thoughts in 2 Pet. 1.10–11 and 3.14.

Do you wish to be able to suffer and yet rejoice? The considerations of heaven and glory will so encourage you that you will be enabled to meet all trials. We see this in Moses, as I have already explained. We see it in the early believers, as we read in Hebrews, chapter 11. To which I might add many more. It is the man who eyes heaven and glory who is able to walk safely in all places. While Peter kept his eye upon Christ, he walked safely upon a stormy and tempestuous sea, but when he took his eye off Christ and looked upon the storminess of the sea, then he began to sink. While we have an eye upon eternals, we are able to walk on the most tempestuous sea, and to go through any storms and troubles; but if once we take our eye off Christ and Heaven, then the least trouble is more than we can bear. It was said by Basil: 'I care for nothing, visible or invisible, if I may but get Christ. Let fire, let the cross, let breaking of bones come, nay, let the torments of the devil come upon me, if only I can get Christ.' Such a blessed enlargement of heart did the consideration of Christ and heaven put into him, that he was able to slight and condemn all the evils of the world. This much is certain, that he who considers the eternal weight of glory will not think the light afflictions, which are but for a moment, worthy to be compared to it. He that sees visions of glory will be like Stephen, who was able to endure a shower of stones. He that considers eternity as the goal to which he moves, does not dread to go through all the troubles of the way. Says Seneca, 'He who keeps eternity in mind does not shrink from the arduousness of the way.'

Would you submit to all God's disposings of your affairs? The considerations of heaven and glory will make the believer submit to any thing here. He can be content to be poor, for he knows he shall be rich; to be reproached, for he knows he shall be honoured; to be afflicted, for he knows he shall be comforted; to be imprisoned, for he knows he shall be brought into a large place; to sit at Dives' door, for he knows he shall rest in Abraham's bosom; to lose all, for he knows he shall find all hereafter. God will be all, and more than all, to him. He knows that the trials last but for a little season, a day, an hour, a moment, a small moment. Hereafter there are eternal embraces. He can submit to God to work His own work, and to work it in His own way, and after His own manner, if so be He will bring him to glory at last. And he can say, Welcome that sorrow that presages joy, that trouble that ends in comfort, those crosses that prepare for crownings, and that death which ushers in eternal life. And all this he can do by the consideration of the great and glorious things which God has reserved for him. Hence we see the necessity of having respect to heaven and glory in our obedience.

8

OBEDIENCE TO MEN

———

QUERY 6 : *Are Christians freed from obedience to men?*

TWO KINDS OF SUBJECTION

Before I answer this query, I must say that some places in Scripture seem to say that it does not stand with Christian liberty to be obedient to men. We find in Scripture (as I showed at the beginning of this treatise) a double charge: 1. That man must not usurp the mastership. 2. That he must not undergo servitude. Thus we read in Matt. 23.9–10: 'Be not ye called Rabbi, for one is your Master, even Christ, and all ye are brethren. And call no man your father upon the earth; for one is your Father, which is in heaven.' Aquinas comments on this verse: 'It is forbidden to men to address rulers as attributing to them a supremacy of rule which enters into rivalry with the rule of God.' We read again in 1 Cor. 7.23: 'Ye are bought with a price; be ye not the servants of men', which indicates that we are not to undergo servitude.

On the other hand, and seemingly in contradiction to this, we read in Rom. 13.1: 'Let every soul be subject to the higher powers. For there is no power but of God; the powers that be are ordained of God.' And again in 1 Pet. 2.13–15: 'Submit yourselves to every ordinance of man for the Lord's sake, whether it be to the king as supreme; or unto governors. . . . As free and not using your liberty for a cloak of maliciousness, but as the servants of God.'

Now how shall we reconcile these two kinds of Scriptures? One says, 'Be ye not the servants of men'; the other says, 'Submit yourselves to every ordinance of man for the Lord's sake'. But the meaning is that we must submit ourselves to the authority of man in such a way that we do not thereby deny our Christian liberty which we have in Christ. And we must maintain our Christian liberty in such a way that we do not, as if making an excuse of our liberty, neglect our Christian duty. Submit yourselves, says the apostle, but as free, not as slaves. As freemen, still submit. He teaches no submission which would contradict Christian freedom.

In brief, then, there is a twofold subjection to man : 1. There is a subjection which may be yielded with the preservation of our Christian liberty; 2. There is a subjection which cannot be yielded without a denial of it. The first of these is implied in the verses just quoted from Romans and 1 Peter, the second in the verses from Matthew and 1 Corinthians. The one pertains to the subjection of the outward man in things lawful; the other pertains to the subjection of the inward man, the soul and conscience, and in things unlawful. The one is a subordinate subjection, a subjection in subordination to God, and so 'for the Lord's sake', as Peter says. The other is an absolute subjection, a subjection of our souls and consciences, for man's sake. To man's authority we may be subject in respect of the outward man in things lawful. But for our souls and consciences, we have no fathers and masters, but only our Father and Master in heaven.

We see both of these positions plainly if we compare Matt. 23.10 with Eph. 5.7. The one reads : 'Be not ye called masters, for one is your Master, even Christ'; and the other : 'Servants, be obedient to your masters according to the flesh'. The distinction is here made between masters according to the flesh and masters according to the spirit. The former appertain to the outward man in outward things. But on earth we have no masters according to the spirit, none to whom we are to subject our souls and consciences, but only Christ. As, in this sense, we have no father, so we have no master upon earth.

OBEDIENCE TO THE CIVIL MAGISTRATE

But it may be objected: Is it not lawful for a magistrate to impose actions upon men which concern their consciences? I answer: It is not lawful for a magistrate to impose anything upon a Christian which it would not be lawful in the eyes of God for him to obey; that is, to set up an authority against Christ's authority, the power of man against the power of God. But a magistrate may require those things at our hands which are clearly revealed to be the will of God. In this we obey God in man, and not so much man as God. In this case we may say as the Samaritans said: 'Now we believe, not because of thy sayings, but because we have heard him ourselves.'

I conceive there may be a distinction drawn between supreme masters and subordinate masters; and between subjection rendered to a master who is himself subject to another, and obedience rendered to one who is supreme and absolute. Those are subordinate masters whom we obey in order that we may obey a higher authority; and those are supreme masters in whom obedience rests and in whom it is finally resolved. The Romish doctrine requires absolute submission to the authority of the Church, an authority which neither men nor angels may usurp without high treason to Jesus Christ. Says Bellarmine: 'You are ignorant and unskilled; therefore if you wish to be saved, there is no other course open to you but to render a blind obedience to our authority.' We repeat that it is treason for any to usurp this authority and wickedness for any to yield to it. If God will not allow a supreme master, neither absolute obedience, in temporal things, but requires us to serve men in subordination to Christ (Eph. 6.7 and Col. 3.23–24), much less will He allow of a supreme master in spiritual things. Certainly it is the highest piece of slavery and vassalage in the world to yield up our consciences to the will of any man, or surrender our judgments to be wholly disposed by the sentences and determinations of others. But in the other sense I conceive that men may be masters, and that we may be subject to them in subordination to God and Christ.

If we look into the Old Testament we find that it plainly sets forth the subordinate character of obedience in things spiritual. The people were bound to obey the magistrates when they commanded obedience to that which God had commanded, and to obey them, not as they were types of Christ, but as they were temporal magistrates and were set to defend the worship of God. Some have imagined that the power of magistrates, leading up to Christ, was to cease when Christ came, who is the great King of His Church, and in whom alone all authority over His people was to be confined, but I do not conceive it so. I conceive that a magistrate, without any trespassing on the authority of Christ, or infringement of the liberty of conscience of the Christian, may require those things to be obeyed which are clearly revealed to be the will and mind of Christ. Yet in this he is but a subordinate, and Christ is the supreme Master. The magistrate tells us what is God's will, not what is his will. He tells us it is his will, too, but only because it is God's will first.

But it may be objected again that, though a magistrate may command or impose things which are clearly evident to be the mind of Christ, yet it is possible for him to seek to impose things of more doubtful obligation. I answer that it should be inquired whether the things imposed are doubtful in themselves, or only doubtful to me. If indeed they be doubtful in themselves, I humbly conceive, either that they should not be imposed at all, or else imposed with all tenderness. But if they be only doubtful to me, they may yet be lawfully imposed, though as yet not lawfully obeyed by me.

My meaning is this: As some things may be lawfully obeyed,

which may not be lawfully imposed, so there are some things which may be lawfully imposed, and yet not lawfully obeyed. Hezekiah's command to break the brazen serpent when he found men idolizing it, was a lawful command which might be lawfully imposed; and yet, if there had been some who had reverential thoughts of it, as a thing which had been set up by God, which had been famous in the wilderness, and moreover which was a type of Christ, and who therefore doubted whether it was right to obey the king's command, I say, in this case it could not have been lawfully obeyed by such, even though the destruction of the brazen serpent was lawfully commanded by Hezekiah.

Certainly, there are many things which may be commanded; and if we have respect merely to the things commanded, they may be lawfully obeyed; but if we have respect to the person who is required to obey, it may be unlawful to him to obey. In this case a man may both sin in doing, for he has an evil conscience in the matter, and he may sin in not doing, for he is guilty of disobedience.

We might become involved in a great dispute on this subject, which it is not my intention to do at this time. It may be possible in some other discourse to treat more largely upon it, and to endeavour to give a satisfactory answer to the multitude of scruples and objections in which this subject, almost more than any other, abounds. But as I have now answered the main queries which have been raised and which are in controversy concerning Christian freedom, I shall conclude the whole with a brief application.

9

THE APPLICATION TO BELIEVERS
AND UNBELIEVERS

If it is the case that Christ has purchased freedom for believers only, and brought believers and them only into the possession of such a privilege, then what must be the fearful condition of unbelievers. You are still in bondage to sin and Satan and the law of God, and who can express a more miserable condition than this.

THE MISERABLE BONDAGE OF THE UNBELIEVER

(i) *To sin*

You are in bondage to sin, not only in bondage by reason of sin, nay, but delivered up to all evils, spiritual, temporal, and eternal. You are under the command of every lust. Every sin is a tyrant in the soul. Christ tells us that whosoever commits sin is the servant of sin (John 8.34). First a man entertains sin as his friend, and afterwards it becomes his master. You are the servants of sin (Rom. 6.20). You are sold under sin, as the apostle explains in reference to his own natural condition (Rom. 7.14). He says, 'I am carnal, sold under sin'. Indeed, we are all of us sold under sin by nature, but here we sell ourselves to sin. As it was said of Ahab, that he 'sold himself to work wickedness', so it may be said of us. We are not only passively content to be vassals of sin, but we actively endeavour to bring ourselves into vassalage. We are actively willing to be sin's slaves rather than to be God's servants. It is set down in Scripture as the character of a man in his natural condition, that he is disobedient, serving divers lusts and pleasures (Titus 3.3). His obedience to sin is not forced, but free, not involuntary but natural and with delight. Hence it is said that sin reigns in natural men. Sin exercises a sovereignty, not a tyranny, in them. They are the professed servants to sin (2 Pet. 2.19), like those men who chose their masters after the Lord's jubilee was proclaimed and whose ears were bored in token of their willingness to be in perpetual subjection.

Such is your state. You are in bondage to sin, and it is a fearful bondage indeed. It is soul slavery. The condition of the Israelites under Pharaoh, and of those who are now prisoners in Turkish galleys, is very sad, but that is but the bondage of the body. But this is a soul slavery, bondage of the soul. What is it to have our bodies in vassalage and our estates enslaved in comparison with the bondage of the soul? Better to be under the tyranny of the most imperious man, than under the vassalage and slavery of sin and our own corruptions. This is the ultimate, the finishing stroke of God, when He gives up a man to the dominion of his sins. 'He that is filthy, let him be filthy still' is the worst of all judgments.

And again, it is a senseless slavery, that is, a slavery we are not conscious of. We say in natural things that those diseases are most mortal that deprive us of sense. And such is the slavery of sin. We are in chains and feel it not; we are under the weight of sin and are not conscious of it. God often brings men into bondage by sin, clapping them under the fears and terrors of an accusing conscience, and all this that He might deliver them from sin's bondage. We say that a burning fever is more hopeful than a state of lethargy. A physician sometimes brings his patient into a state of fever to cure lethargy. Just so, a wounded and troubled conscience is better than a secure and dead conscience. When the strong man keeps the house, all is at peace. Such is the misery of this bondage, that a man is unconscious of the bondage.

Further, it is an active slavery. A man held by his lusts will drudge or take any pains to satisfy them. He will spend his strength, his health, his estate, and endure pain, to satisfy his lusts, though such a man thinks anything too much that is laid out for God and Christ. But nothing is too much to spend on his lusts. Thus is it an active slavery.

It is also a willing slavery. The man counts his slavery freedom, his bondage liberty, his chains of brass to be chains of pearl. The man is of his own will a servant to sin. How often has the Lord's jubilee been sounded in his hearing! How often has Christ been tendered to him to set him free! Yet he chooses to return to his old master. It is therefore a righteous thing with God that he should bore the man's ears in token of eternal slavery to sin and Satan.

And again, it is a bondage from which a man cannot by his own power deliver himself. He cannot redeem himself by price, nor can he deliver himself by power or by conquest. A man may be in bondage to men and yet able to ransom himself, if not from his own resources, yet by the helps and collections and contributions of others. But no man can redeem his own soul. Nay, all the contributions of men and angels fall too short. They have but oil to keep their own lamps alight (Matt. 25.9). It is set down as not only the proper work of Christ, but as the greatest work which Christ has done, to redeem His people from sin. Indeed He did it by price (Gal. 4.5). He bought His people back, but it was not by silver and gold, as Peter tells us; the redemption of their souls is more precious (Ps. 49.7–8), and it was by the blood of Christ.

Nor can the people of God redeem themselves by power. To be a sinner and to be without strength are one and the same thing, in the apostle's phrase (Rom. 5.6–8). And therefore he tells us: 'While we were sinners and without strength, Christ died for us.' Indeed we could do nothing to help ourselves out of this bondage. We were not able to weep, to pray, to work ourselves out of this condition. It is with us as with men caught in quick-sands; the more they strive, the deeper they sink into them. So the more we strive in our own strength and by our own power, the more we become entangled, and the stronger the chain becomes which binds us to this condition. Thus you may get a glimpse into the nature of this miserable state. But this is not all.

(ii) *Bondage to Satan*

You are in bondage to Satan, not that you owed him any-thing—you were only indebted to God's justice—but he is God's jailer, who holds poor souls down as under brazen bars and behind iron gates not to be broken. If a man is in bon-dage it is some relief to him to have a merciful jailer. But this adds to the misery of the sinner, that he has a cruel jailer. The jailer of hell is like Nebuchadnezzar who will take no rewards; he will not be bribed; he cannot be persuaded to set the soul free. Satan is a cruel tyrant who rules in the hearts of the children of disobedience (Eph. 2.2). The sinner is taken captive at his will, as the apostle tells us (2 Tim. 2.26).

Yet some are more royal slaves than others. Some he keeps in close custody. He holds them down with many weights and chains, under the raging power of many lusts and corruptions. Others he keeps in an easier custody, and allows them to be prisoners at large. He suffers them to walk about. They have the liberty of the prison. But yet they are imprisoned at his pleasure and taken captive at his will. He may permit them to do many things—Herod to hear, Judas to preach—yet he holds them by their lusts, and can bring them to heel when he pleases.

Such then is your bondage to Satan. It is a cruel, merciless bondage, to which the bondage of Israel under Pharaoh is not worthy to be compared. It is a universal bondage, universal in respect of persons, for all men are born slaves, and universal in respect of parts, for all parts of a man are involved in it. No part is free. The judgment, the will, the affections, the mind, and the conscience are all in chains, all enslaved to Satan. It is universal also in respect of acts and performances. A sinner in bondage cannot perform one act as a free man. He is required to perform the actions of a free man, such actions as free men do; but he cannot perform them as a free man. He prays as a slave, not as a son. He weeps as a slave, not as a free man. He acts more from fear of the lash, than for hatred of sin and love of God. All his acts are acts in bondage. His very spirit is in bondage. He has no spirit of freedom. And in this sad condition he remains until Christ sets him free.

(iii) *Bondage to the law of God*

Furthermore, such a man is in bondage to the law of God, that is, to its curse and its rigour. The penalties and forfeitures of the law attach to him, as the apostle states in Gal. 3.10: 'As many as are of the works of the law are under the curse'. And why so? 'For it is written, Cursed is every one that does not continue in all things which are written in the book of the law to do them.' And that is impossible to him. Therefore of necessity he is under the curse.

I will take the curse to pieces, as it were, and show what lies within it. It is a comprehensive curse, a universal curse. A man under it is cursed in every condition, in his gold and silver, and in his relations, yea, in his very mercies. Where others are blessed in their afflictions, he is cursed in his mercies. As there is a blessing hid in the worst of things to the godly, in their crosses and losses and in death itself, so there is a curse in the best of things for the wicked man, in his wealth, in his comforts, and in his enjoyments. It is an extensive curse.

It is also an unavoidable curse. Man is born heir to it as surely as he is born a son of Adam. It is an unsupportable curse, which neither men nor angels are able to bear. The angels who have fallen lie under it, and cannot help themselves. The wrath of man may be borne, or at least undergone. It is a wrath that reaches to the body. But who can bear the wrath of God? This is a wrath that reaches to the soul, and who knows, much less who can bear, the power of His wrath?

It is an unremovable curse, so far as we look to anything we can do of ourselves to remove it. If God lays it on a man, not all the power and wit of men and angels can take it off. As none can pluck believers out of the hands of God's mercy, so none can pluck unbelievers out of the hands of His justice. Thus you are in bondage to the curse of the law.

Then, too, you are in bondage to the rigour of the law. It is rigorous in that it requires hard things, difficult things. If you look over the duties commanded, you will find them so. Indeed, you will find them impossible things, as related to the state in which you find yourself. It is a yoke which neither our fathers nor we were able to bear (Acts 15.10). We might as well be set to move mountains, to stop the sun from running his course, to fetch yonder star from heaven, as to do what the law commands. And yet all this it requires to be done by us in the exactness and according to the exactness of the command. It requires perfect obedience, both in respect of the principle, in respect of the manner, and in respect of the end, and it will abate nothing. And all this it requires in our own persons. It will not admit of obedience by a surety. Performance on our behalf by a substitute is Gospel, not law. The law requires all to be done, with the utmost exactness, in our own person (Gal. 3.10).

Nor will the law accept of the most earnest endeavours if there is any failure anywhere in the performance. It will not allow of desires instead of deeds, or of endeavours instead of performance. Desires and endeavours belong not to the law but to the Gospel. And the law requires constancy in its fulfilment; it requires obedience from the whole man of the whole law for the whole of life. If you obey for never so many years and yet fail in one tittle at the last, even if only in a thought or some inclination of the mind, all the obedience counts for nothing. For the law says: 'Cursed is he that does not continue to obey in every thing'.

Notwithstanding all this exaction from a man, yet the law will not afford him any strength or suffer him to get help from another. He must bear his burden alone. The law lays loads on him; it imposes duty without considering his strength; nor will the law afford him strength. It bids a man look for that where he can. It requires performance in strength without giving a man strength to perform.

This, too, shows the rigour of the law, that upon the least failing, all the hopes you may have had of getting good by the law are gone. You are rendered helpless and incapable of ever expecting good from the law. You are undone for ever. Upon Adam's first sin, all his hopes of life by the law ended, and if God had not introduced a Saviour he would have been lost for ever. But some one may say: Might he not have been able to do twice as much good as he had done evil, and so made amends for his former fault? Not at all, for when once a man has offended, if only in the least particular, he can never make amends for it. He can never outdo the law. If he could outdo what the law required, yet all he could do would never make amends, or make up for the former fault. If you were to go about to redeem every idle word by an age of prayers, every act of injustice with a treasury of alms, every omission of duty by millions of duties, yet all this would be too little. It could not possibly make amends for the former failing.

But you will say, Why? What then? Will not the law accept of my tears, my repentance for my fault? No! Here is the further rigour of the law, that if ever you have offended though in the least particular, it will accept of no attempt at amendment. It admits of no place of repentance. It will not admit of tears. Repentance is brought in under the Gospel, not under the law. If you fail in one small thing, and shed seas of tears, even tears of blood; if you weep your eyes out of your head, yet all this is unavailing, for the law admits of no repentance.

Thus it is seen how miserable a thing it is to be under sin's bondage. I have enlarged on the matter so as to commend the great privilege of a Christian's freedom by contrast with it. It is commonly said that contraries illustrate one another, and certainly the sight of the misery of bondage enables the Christian to conceive the better of the blessedness of the freedom which comes through Christ. And this freedom I have explained at length in the earlier part of my discourse, showing how it includes freedom from sin, Satan, and from the law.

THE DUTY OF THE BELIEVER

(i) *To maintain Christian liberty*

But yet again: It is the work of those whom Christ has brought into the enjoyment of this high and glorious privilege to maintain it: 'Stand fast in the liberty wherewith Christ hath made us free' (Gal. 5.1). There are two chief things which Christ has entrusted to us, and we are to preserve them inviolate. The first is Christian faith: 'See that ye earnestly contend for the faith which was once delivered unto the saints' (Jude 3). The second is Christian liberty: 'Stand fast in the liberty wherewith Christ hath made us free'. Every man should be faithful in those things which are entrusted to him, and God has entrusted the Christian man with precious things. Christian faith and Christian liberty are alike precious, and how careful we should be to maintain them! Civil liberties and liberty to go where we will are very precious. How much we engage ourselves just now[1] in defence of our liberties and freedoms against those who would deprive us of them! And indeed they may justly be esteemed men of abject minds who would on any account at all forego their freedoms and liberties.

Leo the Emperor drew up a severe constitution, in which he

[1] The reference is to the first Civil War (Parliament *v.* Charles I), 1642–5.

forbade all men the buying, and all men the selling, of their freedom, esteeming it madness in any man to part with his freedom. And if civil freedom is so precious and is to be maintained, how much more is spiritual freedom, the freedom wherewith Christ makes a man free! A freedom dearly purchased by the blood of Christ! We esteem our civil freedom the better as we remember that it cost so much of the blood of our ancestors to obtain it. It would be baseness in us to be careless of that which cost them their blood. How much more then should we esteem our freedom which was purchased by the precious blood of Christ! You are redeemed, not by silver and gold, but by the blood of Christ, says the apostle. Our freedom is dearly bought, mercifully revealed, freely bestowed, and fully conveyed to us by the Spirit of Christ. We have many and great reasons therefore for maintaining it, and for keeping ourselves clear of the yoke of bondage.

Maintain your liberty in Christ by refusing to look any more to the law for justification, and by refusing to fear its words of condemnation. You are to live, in respect of your practice and obedience, as men who can neither be condemned by the law nor justified by it. It is a hard lesson to live above the law, and yet to walk according to the law. But this is the lesson a Christian has to learn, to walk in the law in respect of duty, but to live above it in respect of comfort, neither expecting favour from the law in respect of his obedience nor fearing harsh treatment from the law in respect of his failings. Let the law come in to remind you of sin if you fall into sin, but you are not to suffer it to arrest you and drag you into the court to be tried and judged for your sins. This would be to make void Christ and grace. Indeed Christians too much live as though they were to expect life by works, and not by grace. We are too big in ourselves when we do well, and too little in Christ in our failings. O that we could learn to be nothing in ourselves in our strength, and to be all in Christ in our weakness! In a word, let us learn to walk in the law as a rule of sanctification, and yet to live upon Christ and the promises in respect of justification.

The law is a yoke of bondage, as Jerome calls it. They who look for righteousness from it are like oxen in the yoke, which draw and toil, and when they have performed their labour, they are fatted for the slaughter. Likewise, when men have endeavoured hard after their own righteousness, they perish at last in their just condemnation. As I have previously said, Luther calls them the devil's martyrs. They take much pains to go to hell. 'They being ignorant of God's righteousness, and going about to establish their own righteousness, have not submitted themselves to the righteousness of God' (Rom. 10.3). Proud nature would fain do something for the purchase of glory. God will have it to be of grace, and man would have it of debt. God will have it to be of gift, and man would have it of purchase. We have too much of this nature in us. We go to prayer and look upon our duties and our tears as so much good money laid out for the purchase of eternal blessings. Nay, even if we do not bring money, yet we would plead our own qualifications and dispositions as if they were our deservings. This utterly crosses with God's designs. He will have all to be of grace. Man would have all to be of debt. God's word is not now, 'Do this and live', but 'Believe and thou shalt be saved'. Walk in the duties of the law, but with a Gospel spirit. The law is to be acknowledged as a rule of sanctification, but it is to be rejected in respect of justification. It was well said by Luther: 'Walk in the heaven of the promise, but in the earth of the law', that is, in the heaven of the promise, in respect of believing, and in the earth of the law in respect of obeying. In this way the Christian gives the law its honour and Christ His glory.

Maintain your Christian liberty against men, as well as against the law. That liberty is a precious jewel and we must suffer none to rob us of it. Let us never surrender our judgments or our consciences to be at the disposal and opinions of others, and to be subjected to the sentences and determinations of men. We must allow neither power nor policy, neither force nor fraud, to rob us of it.

The apostle says, 'Stand fast and be not entangled'. Let us not return like willing slaves into our former chains. Ambrose has said that it is a greater evil for a freeman to be made a slave than for a man to be born into slavery. The believer must beware of being tempted into slavery, as the fish is enticed into the net. He must take heed that he is not ensnared and overwhelmed by the policies of men. We are warned in the Word to take heed that none deceive us (Eph. 5.6; 2 Cor. 4.8; 2 Thess. 2.3), as if it were in our power to prevent it. And so it is! We can only be ensnared by our own fault. We often betray away our liberty when we might maintain it; and thus we become the servants of men.

This fault arises either from weakness of head, or from wickedness of heart. It is my exhortation therefore to all Christians to maintain their Christian freedom by constant watchfulness. You must not be tempted or threatened out of it; you must not be bribed or frightened from it; you must not let either force or fraud rob you of it. To what purpose is it to maintain it against the Papists, who are the open enemies of it, and against others who would take it from us, and yet give it up to them by our own hands, yea, to them perhaps who do not seek it from us? Nothing is more usual. We must therefore beware. We must not give up ourselves to the opinion of other men, though they be never so learned, never so holy, merely because it is their opinion. The apostle directs us to try all things and to hold fast that which is good (1 Thess. 5.21). It often happens that a high esteem of others in respect of their learning and piety makes men take up all upon trust from such, and to submit their judgments to their opinions, and their consciences to their precepts. This should not be so. Men will suspect a truth if a liar affirms it. For this reason Christ would not own the devils' acknowledgment of Him, when they said, 'Thou art the Son of God'. But men are ready to believe an error, to give credit to an untruth, if an honest and faithful man affirms it. Whatever such a man says comes with a great deal of authority into men's spirits. Yet it is possible for such men to be mistaken.

It is a most dangerous thing to have men's persons in too much admiration, as we are warned in Jude 16. We know but in part (1 Cor. 13.12). The best are imperfect in knowledge. For the most learned and for the holy martyrs we must make due allowance. They are but men, and thereby they are liable to err, though it may be granted that, since they are learned and holy, it is highly probable that what they speak is truth. But learning and holiness are not infallible evidences. There is much heed to be given to learned and holy men, but we are not to tie our boat to their ship, or, as the phrase is, pin our faith upon their sleeves. We must not subject our judgments, and rest our faith, upon their authority. This would be to make men masters of our faith. This would be a thread of that garment whereby Babylon is distinguished, a mark of the antichristian Church of Rome. It would cause our faith to rest upon the authority of men. This is not to be our practice, though I grant that it is done (though more finely done) by many, even as by those Papists of whom implicit faith and blind obedience are required.

Suffer the continued work of exhortation. It is your duty to labour to maintain Christian freedom. It was dearly purchased for you and mercifully bestowed on you, and therefore should not be weakly lost. Nor should it be maintained in a wilful way. It was given in mercy and must be kept in judgment. We must use the judgment of discretion in rejecting or embracing doctrines. We are neither blindly to subject ourselves to them, no matter how holy and learned they may be who teach them, nor are we to reject them perversely. So much, then, by way of the second part of this exhortation. But there is still something more.

(ii) Not to abuse Christian liberty

Beware of abusing our liberty in Christ. Christian liberty is a precious thing; and the more precious, the more care is needed not to abuse it. Precious things are usually commended to us with words of caution. That I may not speak into the air, I must say that there are various ways in which Christian liberty may be abused. We abuse it when, in the use of it, we cause grief to others. Liberty was purchased for the comfort of ourselves, not for the afflicting of others. They abuse it who so use it as to grieve others. We read of some young Christians at Corinth who ate meat offered to idols, for the sole purpose of showing their liberty. But the apostle tells them: 'All things are lawful for me, but all things are not expedient' (1 Cor. 10.24). The same apostle is frequent in instructing Christians how to exercise their liberty without causing scandal. 'Brethren, ye have been called unto liberty; only use not liberty for an occasion to the flesh, but by love serve one another' (Gal. 5.13). Christ has taken off our former yoke of bondage, not that we should be more wanton, but more careful. It is indeed for our comfort that He has done it, but not to destroy others, as the apostle argues in 1 Cor. 8.11: 'Through thy knowledge shall the weak brother perish, for whom Christ died'.

But I will hasten to a conclusion, so will include all else in a final brief word. There is another way in which we may abuse Christian liberty, and that is, when we use it to admit superstition. Many will say they have Christian liberty, and therefore dare venture upon any observances, customs, and practices, although never warranted by the Word. This indeed is Christian licentiousness, not Christian liberty. Christian liberty is a liberty bounded by laws and rules. Those who do away with all such bounds are therefore libertines.

We abuse Christian liberty when we make void the law of God, as I have already shown at length; when we judge it our liberty to be exempted from duty. This is true bondage rather than true liberty. The liberty of a believer lies not in exemption from service, but in service; and surely that man is yet in bondage who does not judge service to be his liberty.

We also abuse our liberty when we give too much scope to ourselves in things that are lawful. It is an easy thing to run from use to abuse. Of such men Jude speaks in the fourth verse of his epistle: 'There are certain men . . . who turn the grace of our God into wantonness'. We also abuse it when we use it undutifully, denying obedience to lawful authority in things lawful, upon pretence of Christian liberty; which is tantamount to the overthrowing of all lawful authority. We abuse it also when we will be tied to nothing but what our own spirits incline us to. Of this, too, I have spoken at large, and therefore I shall conclude with the words of the apostle in 1 Pet. 2.16: 'You are free, but use not your liberty for a cloak of maliciousness, but as the servants of God.'